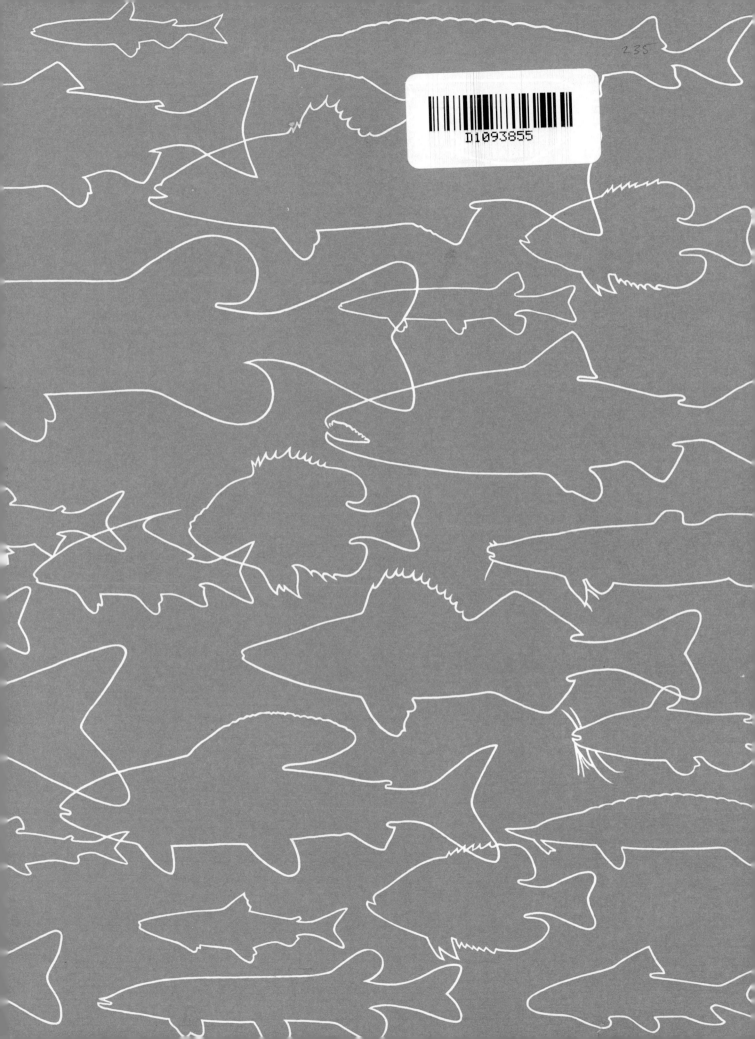

235

FISH and FISHING

FISH and FISHING

Written and illustrated by
Maynard Reece

a Better Homes & Gardens Book

MEREDITH PRESS

NEW YORK   DES MOINES

Contents

Introduction

Increasing leisure time, easy-to-use equipment, and advanced modes of transportation have combined to help make fishing a major participation sport for the family. As more and more people are joining in the fun, we felt that a book should be written for those who are looking for a one-volume authority on fresh-water angling.

Award-winning wildlife artist-author Maynard Reece, himself an adept hunter and fisherman, is one of the few men in the country who could not only write such a book but also illustrate it. Mr. Reece traveled over 50,000 miles to collect this information, painting the fish from living specimens to assure accuracy in every detail.

Such a book cannot be written by one person alone. American and Canadian naturalists and scientists, biologists of state and federal agencies, and anglers throughout North America have added immensely to its completeness. Special thanks and credit go to Doctor Reeve M. Bailey, Curator of Fishes, University of Michigan, for providing technical assistance in the presentation of 80 familiar species of fresh-water fishes.

The Editors

Chapter **1**

Where to go fishing

Seven vacation trips for the entire family

Let's go fishing. Whether fishing a local pond for bluegill or a distant mountain stream for cutthroat trout, few sports combine so many pleasures as those enjoyed by fishermen. Relaxing amid spectacular North American scenery makes such a trip worth-while even without catching fish. But add the intrigue of matching wits with a wily adversary, the skill of a good cast, and the sudden explosion of lightning activity, and you have the ingredients for an unforgettable family fishing vacation.

Fortunately, few anglers in North America need to travel long distances to catch one or more species of fish. None-theless, within most fishermen lies the urge to sample new waters and to try a variety of angling techniques. Ease of transportation into areas where a particular species of fish is available makes fulfilling such desires a simple matter.

The seven family fishing trips we will suggest combine the possibility of wonderful fishing with magnificent scenery. Some trips are new variations of an old idea, made possible today because of modern equipment and new fishing facilities. Certain of these trips are for the budget minded, and all are designed to appeal to the diversified interests of fishermen and their families.

← *This family picked the Teton Mountain area, Wyoming, for a fishing trip*

Auto trip

Resorts, trailer and tent camping

Each year fishermen and their families depend upon the automobile more than any other mode of transportation to get them to favorite fishing areas. It's economical, relatively fast, and allows a reasonable degree of mobility for other forms of relaxation when fishing is slow.

But in most cases a car, or even a station wagon, cannot provide comfortable housing for an entire family. Generally the fishing family faces one of three choices for shelter: they can check in at a resort, tow a trailer, or carry camping equipment.

There are thousands of excellent resorts in North America's best fishing areas. Many of these cater only to fishermen, others combine fishing with other activities for families. Staying at a good resort has important advantages to the fisherman. He will find dependable boats and motors for rent, the service of a guide if desired, plus reliable fishing information from the resort owner.

Good resorts, located as far north as Great Bear Lake on the Arctic Circle, take many of the discomforts out of fishing. A cabin or fishing lodge will usually put you in the company of other fishermen: few anglers are so expert that they can't learn something new from other sportsmen around a fireplace.

Trailer camping increases in popularity each year. Trailer parks are springing up all over North America, many in the heart of good fishing areas. These parks supply parking space for the trailer, electricity, running water, and often a playground for the youngsters.

The lack of a trailer park in the vicinity he wishes to fish is of little concern to the trailer camper. For the more adventurous family willing to sacrifice a few luxuries, trailer space can be found near many good fishing lakes and streams. And when fishing gets slow or the other side of the hill beckons, he can always move on.

Tent camping is the universal means by which anglers set up housekeeping in fishing country. Today literally thousands of well-kept campgrounds are within range of the family car. Modern, lightweight camping equipment minimizes many of the discomforts once akin to outdoor living. But the primary asset of tent camping lies in its mobility. If fishing is mediocre in one location, it's a simple matter to break camp, throw the gear in the car trunk, or car-top carrier, and drive to another area.

Trailer camping

Trailers, pick-up trucks with mounted camper bodies, and sports bus-wagons require little set-up time once they reach the camp site. Improved roads in many excellent fishing areas, plus light, comfortable, and easily maneuvered equipment are responsible for increased trailer camping among anglers. A trailer rental agency can supply equipment.

Tent camping

Some of the best fishing and scenery in the world is accessible to the tent camper. These anglers set up a snug camp before going after trout in Montana's Canyon Ferry Lake. Station wagons in camping country are used extensively for sleeping and cooking as well as for transportation. Tent camping is one of the least expensive fishing trips.

Resort living

←—Staying at a resort allows the angler to devote his full attention to fishing rather than bothering about camp chores. If the fish aren't biting, or the weather suddenly turns bad, most fishing resorts offer a number of other activities for their guests.

Take your boat along

Many fishermen take their boats with them on an auto fishing trip. Boat launching areas are increasing in number, some give the fishermen access to relatively unfished waters. Be sure to check local boating laws before launching your boat.

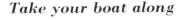

Hiking is exhilarating, especially with large fish waiting at your destination

Hiking trip

There are few less expensive ways to enjoy a family fishing adventure than to get out of the car at the end of the road and hike to a secluded lake or stream. Getting off the beaten path almost always insures better fishing, for streams and lakes close to highways or country roads are usually the most heavily fished.

Before hiking to a secluded lake or stream for a day's fishing, a family should take time to do a bit of planning. Inexperienced hikers miss much of the fun if they go loaded down like a pack horse. But, if they don't take necessary items, they may not enjoy the hike.

Hikers should carry only the bare fishing essentials. One rod and reel apiece, or less than that if they want to take turns fishing. It isn't necessary to carry a tackle box. Fishermen generally select a few lures that have proved themselves in the past and let it go at that. A small screwdriver and a pair of pliers, as well as a

pocketknife, are always handy to have along.

Don't forget lunch. Hiking makes for hearty appetites. Each member of the family can carry his own lunch in a cloth sack tied to his belt, or lunch for everyone will easily fit in a small knapsack. To be on the safe side, it's a good idea for hikers to carry their own drinking water. Two-quart canteens per day are usually sufficient for a party of four.

Wise anglers take along a good insect repellent and hope that they won't have to use it. Matches in a waterproof container are always a good safety measure. A small pocket-size first aid kit is a must. Families should be sure to check with their forest service for campfire regulations. Be certain campfires are extinguished.

Each member of the family must wear sturdy shoes, preferably boots, that have been broken in before they set off through the woods. Rest stops each hour help reduce fatigue.

Flying trip

Airplane travel opens some of the greatest fishing areas in North America. Areas once accessible only by days or weeks of hard canoeing and many unmarked portages are now reached in a few hours by float-equipped airplanes. Many of these lakes are rarely fished, making the old-timer's stories of "a fish on every cast" a possibility for today's wilderness anglers.

A number of different types of flying-in trips are available to fishermen. The most common trip is to fly to a lodge or fishing camp located far back in the wilderness, accessible only from the air or by a long and tiresome canoe journey with many portages enroute. The trip to a fishing camp is usually a package proposition with the cost of air travel included in the per day charge while at the wilderness camp.

Most of these wilderness camps are completely modern, boasting private cabins with baths, and the latest in boats and motors. Meals in central dining halls are similar in quality to what you would expect at your favorite restaurant. Camp operators pride themselves in providing luxury in the most primitive frontier areas. Experienced guides are available with shore lunches to complement fresh catches of fish which are cooked at noon over the open campfire on shore.

There are a number of wilderness camps now operating in parts of Canada and Alaska, with others being built each year. Once fishermen have arrived by air, most camp operators offer their guests two types of accommodations. The anglers can stay at the main camp and fish surrounding waters during the day, returning to a hot meal and a comfortable bed each evening. Or the alternate plan offered by many camps uses the lodge as a base camp from which to fly into surrounding lakes, there to fish for species not found in abundance in near-by waters.

Accessible only by plane, Plummer's Great Bear Lake Lodge in arctic provides top lake trout, grayling fishing.

Fishermen are ready for big fish minutes after landing on wilderness lake

These anglers are fishing from an easily transported inflatable rubber boat that packs to the size of a small suitcase. Fly-in trips such as this are becoming increasingly popular with fishermen, especially those sportsmen wanting good trout fishing. Some fish such as arctic grayling and arctic char inhabit only wilderness waters. Pilots specializing in fly-in trips usually know which lakes are producing the best catches of a particular species. Fishermen should always be prepared with food and clothing to stay longer than the original time agreed upon with the pilot, in case bad weather causes a delay in plane's return.

Many fishing camp operators have boats located in a number of lakes some distance from the main camp. For a specified charge, fishermen are flown to these lakes, either for a single day's fishing, or for several days. If anglers want to stay away from the main camp overnight, the camp operator will fly in camping equipment and food and return for the party on a selected day. This type of trip appeals to many fishermen because it puts them farther off the beaten path where they can enjoy wilderness camping as well as fishing. Others dislike being limited to one area when facilities are available to satisfy their wanderlust.

Another type of flying-in trip, which costs less than the trips previously mentioned, also combines camping and fishing. There are many planes on the edges of wonderful fishing areas available for charter. It is a simple matter to charter a plane with pilot and be flown into one of a thousand wilderness lakes. Once the anglers have been put down on the lake of their choice, the pilot returns to his base of operations with the understanding that he will pick up the party at the end of a specified period of time.

If fishermen have their own camping equipment and supplies, this type of fly-in trip is especially economical. Camping equipment is usually available from a local outfitter in any case. A canoe can be flown in, lashed to one of the floats on the plane, if the anglers require a boat. But many fishermen solve the boat problem by taking along an inflatable rubber boat, which, depending on its size, will hold 1 to 4 persons, yet folds into a small package.

This type of trip can be for any length of time. In and out the same day is possible if the lake to be fished is not too far from the airplane base. The charge for a wilderness charter trip is usually based on a certain amount per air mile. Since the angler pays only for air travel, a longer stay reduces daily expenses.

Since the useful load a light plane can carry is restricted, weight of equipment is an important consideration when planning a fly-in trip. Fishermen should check over their equipment and tackle carefully prior to the trip, eliminating all but the essentials. Unneeded equipment can raise the cost of a fly-in expedition if the plane has to make an extra trip.

Information regarding trips into specific areas can be obtained from travel agencies or fish and game commissions. Many air line companies operating over wilderness areas offer fly-in trips for fishermen. For anglers wanting true wilderness fishing in the last frontiers of North America, a fly-in trip is the answer.

Fly-in trip paid off with big fish

The beautiful lake trout taken by this angler were the result of a fly-in trip to remote fishing camp in the far north country. Boat and guide as well as food and lodging were furnished by camp operator. The season in some areas near the Arctic Circle is short because water is frozen most of the year.

Houseboat trip

Houseboat trips on lakes and rivers are growing in popularity with fishing families who shy from the rigors of camp life. A floating lodge carries home comforts into remote waters miles from the nearest community. It provides a floating base camp where a family rallies at the end of a day's adventure.

These floating homes are ideal for family fishing vacations. Children especially enjoy the versatility such a vacation offers. If they tire of fishing and swimming, they can always go ashore for exploring. To be able to fish, swim, and explore both on water and land without having to return to a cabin or pitch camp for the night is a relaxing experience for every family member.

Most families will want to try houseboating several times before investing in a boat of their own. Reliable houseboat rental agencies can be located by checking with a state fish and game department, by looking over advertisements in outdoor magazines, or by writing the chamber of commerce in the area in which you wish to vacation.

The rental agency will mail their rates, sizes of boats available, and dates open. They often have several rental plans to choose from; one plan usually includes a combination guide-cook, and supplies. About all a family needs to take is its fishing tackle, clothing, and other personal items. Another type plan puts the family entirely on its own, with the operator furnishing only the boat and gas.

If the family arrives at its departure point

Under way on Rainy Lake, Canada

← While Dad pilots the houseboat from inside the cabin, Mom and the kids on top soak up sunshine and enjoy a view of the lake. This houseboat has a drinking water supply in the "stack" on the cabin roof deck.

and decides not to take along a guide, the houseboat owner will offer a few hours of instruction in piloting the craft. These boats are usually powered with a 25 horsepower or larger outboard motor mounted on the stern. A small outboard motor is carried for emergency use or both motors can be used for greater speed when moving from one area to another.

The pilot wheel and motor controls are inside at the front of the cabin. After a short period of instruction, most people maneuver one of these floating houses without difficulty. The helmsman must always keep in mind, however, that the heavy houseboat will glide for some distance after the motor is shut off. It's best to approach the shore very slowly and use the reverse gear on the motor as a brake.

Navigating on lakes and rivers is not difficult. Accurate maps and basic navigating rules are provided by the houseboat rental agency. Maps of Rainy Lake on the Minnesota-Canada border, for example, show every island, sand bar, submerged rock pile, and water depth. In this popular houseboating lake, buoys mark channels, rocks, and sand bars.

A houseboat floats on a series of airtight metal compartments welded together into two long floats. One or more compartments can be punctured with no danger of the houseboat's sinking; steering remains near normal.

A small fishing boat is usually pulled along behind the houseboat for greater fishing flexibility. When sportsmen reach their destination, the houseboat is piloted into a quiet cove and anchored to shore by means of a cable and winch. The anglers then use the more maneuverable small boat for casting or trolling.

Youngsters especially enjoy casting or still fishing from the houseboat roof deck, but all a conservative adult need do is step out the cabin door and cast his lure. And remember, if the fishing isn't good in one spot, it's a simple matter to bring in the anchor and move the houseboat to another part of the lake.

Good fishing at your own front door

Many families tow a small fishing boat behind their houseboat. Nonetheless, part of the fun of houseboating is being able to fish from your front deck.

Typical houseboat floor plan

The interior arrangement of most houseboats is similar in efficiency to a trailer home. This particular craft accommodates six people comfortably; some sleep eight or more people, others as few as four. The guide-cook usually sleeps in a tent set up on the roof deck. Houseboats are heated, stay snug in bad weather.

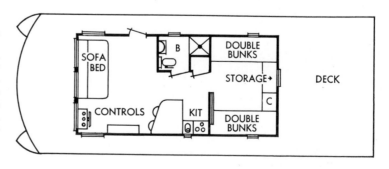

This family found a quiet cove and decided to linger. There's something for everyone to do on a houseboat trip.

Compact galley operates on bottle gas or generator.　　Beachcombing and swimming add variety to trip.

Float trip

Anglers who like their fishing trips slow and relaxed consider floating the ideal sport. This type of trip combines good fishing with a minimum of physical effort. It's possible to take a leisurely one-day float down river or extend the trip for several days and camp overnight on a gravel bar or beach; either way, you fish the entire distance.

A float trip simply means putting a boat in a stream or river and letting the current carry it while the angler fishes hard-to-reach areas seldom tried by shore-bound sportsmen. Many anglers have discovered excellent fishing and spectacular scenery almost at their doorsteps with such an expedition.

Regardless of where the fisherman lives, chances are good that within a short distance of his home there is a river or stream suitable for floating. His state game and fish department can help him locate these waters and in many cases will be able to furnish maps.

After the angler receives the information, he may want to scout on his own by driving as close to the river as possible and as far downstream as he plans to float. It is helpful to know where bridges cross the river, location of gas stations if he carries a motor, and if there are towns along the river where supplies can be purchased. The availability of fresh water for drinking is also important.

Once the angler has decided on the river to float, how far he wants to go, and who will pick him up at the end of the trip, his next consideration is what type of boat to use. Because many parts of the river may be shallow, a boat with a shallow draft is usually the best choice. With this consideration in mind, almost any type of fishing craft will do: wood or metal boats, rubber boats of the life raft type, or canoes.

In some areas of the country special "john" or longboats are especially adaptable for this

Floating down a good bass stream

These fishermen use john boats to reach the seldom →
fished areas of this river. The shallow draft boats
provide stable platforms for anglers. Beautiful scenery
is a bonus feature for float trip fishermen.

type fishing. These flat, wide boats, usually square at bow and stern, are used almost exclusively by float trip outfitters of the White, Current, and Black Rivers in Missouri and Arkansas Ozark area.

Fishermen who have no equipment of their own can often rent everything they need from float trip outfitters scattered throughout the country. Rent for equipment is usually charged on a per-day basis.

Basic equipment for an overnight or longer float trip includes sleeping bags, tent, cooking equipment, food, and drinking water. Personal items such as folding chairs, air mattresses, gasoline stove, portable grill, and ice chest will make the trip more comfortable. You should know how to swim or be willing to wear a life jacket at all times on the water. Youngsters should always wear life jackets when in the boat.

If a trip lasts more than one day, anglers should take time to pick a good camp site each night. A spot at least a few feet above the river level will be drier than immediate beach area, and there's less worry about a sudden rise in the river level if a rainstorm hits during the night. Also, the higher a camp is above the river, the

more breeze is available to help combat insects.

On many streams the fisherman may run into moderately fast water which can be dangerous. Time taken to look over the river is always well spent. If an angler can't be sure what's ahead, he should go ashore and scout downstream. If fast water appears safe to float, the rower should keep the bow of the boat pointed upstream, using the oars to pull up against the current to control the craft. Rocks near the surface will create a white plume of water or a V-shaped ripple on the surface. The rocks are 2 to 3 feet upstream from the plume.

If the sportsman has misgivings about floating his boat through fast water, it's best to play it safe and find another way. The risk of a hole in a boat isn't worth the time an angler might save by floating down fast water. It's always possible to carry the boat around fast water, or get out and wade beside it, guiding it through, or line the boat down. Lining simply means tying a rope to the boat and floating the craft through the fast water while the anglers walk the river bank holding onto the rope. Lining is always tricky, however, and boats and canoes can be swamped in fast water using this method.

Rubber boats, easily packed into remote areas, are practical for floating Montana's swift Flathead River.

These overnight float trip fishermen selected a sandbar camp site in the open and a few feet above water level. Motors are handy for returning upstream, or for hurrying downstream to productive fishing spots.

Canoes are often used for floating because they are light, strong, maneuverable, and have a shallow draft.

A rubber boat carries anglers to remote fishing areas in Idaho and Montana inaccessible by other methods.

Canoe trip

Canoe trips have grown in popularity among fishermen and their families in recent years. Increased fishing pressure on easily reached streams and lakes has pushed sportsmen farther into remote areas for good fishing. For those anglers who don't like crowded fishing conditions and prefer to fish unhurried, where and when the mood strikes them, the canoe trip is a practical answer.

One needn't be an expert in handling a canoe to take a wilderness trip. An angler should, however, practice on a neighboring stream or lake before he sets out on a longer trip into a wilderness area.

In many areas aluminum canoes, with lightweight durable hulls which require little maintenance yet resist sharp snags and rocks, have largely replaced wood and canvas types. Fiberglass holds a promising future for canoes.

Once a person decides to take a canoe trip, several possibilities for implementing the expedition are open to him. If he has his own camping equipment, it will probably fill his needs for a canoe trip. But bear in mind that weight is an important consideration when you portage from one lake to another. Heavy or unnecessary equipment can mean two portage trips instead of one.

People on their first canoe trip often carry more equipment than necessary. But they soon learn that the essentials are limited to a good tent, sleeping bags, outdoor clothing, packsacks, fishing tackle, food, and a canoe with an extra paddle. An outfitter in the area in which you plan to canoe will provide a list of needed equipment to the last detail.

All the family pitches in on portages

Each portage, tree-rimmed lake, or unexplored stream ➞ is an exciting adventure on a canoe trip. Lightweight camping equipment and canoes take much of the work out of transporting gear from one lake to another.

If you haven't camping equipment or a canoe, these items can be rented from him or from a store specializing in camping supplies.

In the famous Quetico-Superior wilderness area which lies along the northern border of Minnesota and southern border of Canada, you have a choice of several reliable outfitters. The outfitter you choose will provide all or any part of the equipment you require. Let him know your needs, how many in your party, how long you plan to stay, and he will have all necessary equipment assembled and ready to go when you arrive. He will provide food or you can buy your own. His charges are usually on a low per-person per-day basis.

The outfitter will spend some time with you going over the maps of the canoeing area. He

A canoe must be loaded carefully

← The weight of equipment should be kept evenly distributed. Bow paddler gets into the canoe first, other occupants next, stern paddler is last to enter.

This family of four carries fishing and camping equipment, plus food for a week's trip in an 18-foot canoe.

will locate camp sites, good fishing spots, and indicate a route suited to your time and interests. If you want to spend all your time fishing and not worry about setting up a camp or cooking, the outfitter can provide a competent guide who will handle these chores.

What kind of canoe trip you take is up to your party. You can map out a route which calls for portaging from lake to lake or stream to stream, or you can usually map a route eliminating portaging altogether. Most canoe enthusiasts like a few portages on their trips and to get far back into wilderness areas, portaging is a necessity.

You can, of course, take a canoe trip anywhere there's available water. The area does not have to be wilderness. Most parts of the

Hang on tight, he's a beauty!

There's no problem in keeping the children entertained on a canoe trip. Fishing, exploring, and swimming make this family expedition go too fast.

At the camp site an overturned canoe makes a handy, clean work counter for necessary housekeeping chores.

Even the smallest anglers have good luck in remote waters reached by canoe

country have streams and lakes suitable for canoeing and canoe trips.

The correct type of food is essential to the success of any canoe trip. If you decide to buy your own food, make a detailed list. It is a smart idea to plan each meal separately. A good bit of weight can be eliminated if you plan carefully. A few cans of soup are a great deal heavier than a package of dry soup ingredients to which you add water. The new freeze-dry foods, which need only to be soaked in water a few minutes before cooking, weigh less than fresh foods. There are also many lightweight dried foods now available with exceptional taste. Choose your food carefully, keep the total weight down, but don't scrimp on quantity. The open air does wonders for appetites.

Special care in packing food will pay dividends at mealtime. Double-wrap loaves of bread so they will stay fresh longer; pack eggs in dry oatmeal or flour to prevent breakage; place butter, catsup, syrup, and other liquids in non-breakable leakproof containers.

All equipment and food should be packed in packsacks provided by outfitters. These are easy to carry on portages and will keep the contents dry when it rains. Fewer loose items means an easier portage. At night, all packsacks should be stored under an overturned canoe for

protection from moisture and marauding bears.

On canoe trips, most anglers fish with artificial lures as carrying live bait for any length of time is a problem. Worms in special bedding will stay alive for some time. The new flexible plastic baits make good substitutes for live baits.

It's best to pack your fishing rods in a sturdy case to prevent damage. One feels a trifle silly with a broken fishing rod in the middle of a wilderness area. Rod cases can be tied onto packs for portages.

Anglers should not try to cover too much water on the first day or two. Muscles not used to canoeing get sore in a short time. It's best to plan an early start each day and stop paddling early in the afternoon. This gives you time to get a comfortable camp set up before dark. It's no fun stumbling around a strange area in the dark looking for tent stakes or an axe.

Probably the greatest enjoyment connected with a canoe trip, next to the excellent fishing, of course, is the freedom to appreciate the beauty of the area. If you decide your camp site is so beautiful you don't want to leave, you can stay there for as long as you like. How you spend your time is strictly up to you, and the hustle and bustle of the "outside" world is easy to forget. Cost-wise, a canoe trip is inexpensive, particularly if you own equipment.

After camp is set up, fishing begins

Many camp sites in canoeing areas are equipped →
with a table and fireplace. When camp chores are
completed, there is usually a rush for the fishing
tackle by young and old alike. Casting from shore
as these youngsters are doing is often productive.

In this Quetico-Superior canoe country of Minnesota and Canada, smallmouth bass, walleye, and
northern pike provide great fishing. A fish dinner is
coming up for these enthusiastic young fishermen.

Casting toward shore paid off

To a youngster, any size fish is a good one if he
can catch it himself, but when that fish is a fair-
sized fighting northern pike the situation sometimes demands help from Dad and the landing net.

When casting from a canoe, or almost any type of
small boat, it is a good idea for no more than two
fishermen to cast at the same time. More than two
anglers casting from the same boat increases beyond safe limits the chance of tangled lines or accidentally hooking a fisherman instead of a fish.

↓

Pack trip

A great many lakes and streams located in remote mountainous areas of the United States and Canada are fished infrequently, if at all, because of their limited accessibility. However, the enterprising angler on a pack trip into the high-mountain country can reach these waters for a never-to-be-forgotten vacation and fishing experience.

You needn't be an expert horseman or angler to go on a pack trip. A good outfitter will furnish well-trained horses and good saddles. You can usually get a list of approved pack trip outfitters from the state chamber of commerce in the area you want to visit, or from the fish and game department of that state.

The outfitter provides all the equipment except personal items necessary for your trip. He will take along one or two wranglers or guides, and a cook if you desire. These men will know the best fishing spots on the lakes and the preferred method of catching fish in that particular area.

Once you have contacted an outfitter and have made the necessary arrangements for your trip, you can insure a pleasant time by horseback riding beforehand. A few miles on a horse for someone not accustomed to riding regularly can be uncomfortable to say the least. It's a good idea to ride for an hour or two every day for a week or more prior to setting off on a mountain pack trip.

Don't exclude the children from your pack trip. Outfitters will see to it that they are assigned gentle horses with saddles of appropriate size. Youngsters love the excitement of this type fishing vacation. Their fishing enthusiasm seldom dwindles because the fish are plentiful and easily caught.

Metal fishing-rod cases are a necessity as your personal equipment will be placed in pack boxes and loaded on a pack horse. A low-hanging limb can snap unprotected rods.

Pack string heads for high country

← Beautiful scenery is one of many rewards of a pack trip. This outfit with camping and fishing gear moves into the Jim Bridger Wilderness Area in Wyoming.

Your clothing should be packed in duffel bags of heavy material capable of withstanding snagging limbs or rubbing against rocks. You should take a good, stout pair of boots as well as a pair of comfortable shoes to wear around camp. A wide-brimmed hat and sun glasses are essential. Sunshine in the high country is penetrating and you will sunburn quickly without protection. Nights in the mountains get chilly so take warm clothing. Your outfitter is a good judge of the type and quantity of clothing you will need.

Most outfitters will want you to arrive at their base of operations a day early to give them a chance to determine how many pack horses

Wranglers load pack horses

← Equipment and food fit into pack boxes or *panniers*. Each horse carries two panniers, plus gear on top.

Pack trip members gather at cook's tent for breakfast at this wilderness camp

Tepee tents to the left of the cook tent are sleeping quarters for the guests; two to a tent. The cook tent doubles as a warm loafing spot as well as for cooking and eating in bad weather. Situated beside a clear lake packed with trout, this snug camp becomes the base of operations for daily treks in the wilderness.

your personal gear will require. Arriving early also gives the outfitter a chance to choose horses and saddles for each member of your party.

You can plan as long or as short a trip as you choose. You can move camp every day or do as most pack outfits do: set up a base camp high in the mountains and take short day-long side trips to near-by lakes. This latter method gives you more fishing time since you aren't breaking and setting up camp each day.

In some areas, you can make arrangements with an outfitter to pack you and your camping equipment into an area and leave you there for a specified number of days. The outfitter will provide the necessary equipment or you can use your own. You may want to keep a riding horse for each member of the party when the outfitter leaves with the pack horses.

On trail to a remote mountain lake

These fishermen have left their base camp for a day's → fishing in a high mountain lake. The single pack horse trails behind carrying lunch, fishing equipment. Party will start back in time to avoid riding after dark.

Above timber line, anglers assemble their fishing rods in preparation for golden trout fishing in a near-by lake.

Teaching children fishing techniques is easy when they see in crystal water the effect of their actions upon the fish.

This type of trip is less expensive than when an outfitter remains with you during your stay in the mountains. You can employ a cook to stay with you or do your own cooking. Accurate maps are available for most areas to prevent your getting lost if you take side trips from your base camp.

For high mountain fishing you can use a fly rod, spinning tackle, or casting equipment. Dry flies, wet flies, spinners, and small wobbling lures are effective. You have a choice of cutthroat, rainbow, brook, or golden trout fishing, depending upon the area of the country selected for your trip.

The next time you decide you want to try something entirely different in the way of a family fishing trip, give serious consideration to a high country pack trip. It will be an experience you'll remember around a fire on many a cold winter evening.

Wilderness lunch of deep-fried trout

← It's hard to beat the flavor of fresh-caught trout cooked over an open fire. Brookies were cleaned, head and skin removed, then deep-fried in hot butter. Result: tender brook trout at their mild-flavored best.

A quick, refreshing wash ↑

It's wash-up time before lunch for these youngsters who rode, with their parents, from a base camp for a day's fishing. Water in most high country lakes is crystal clear and safe to drink. Riding, fishing, and exploring keep children busy.

In this quiet mountain lake youngsters used spinning tackle, small metal lures for cutthroat trout.

Stream fishing pays off

Many high country anglers neglect → to fish the small streams connecting mountain lakes. These areas can produce good catches of cutthroat and rainbow trout as this youngster demonstrates.

Streams are good spots for children to fish, as long, accurate casts aren't as important as in lake fishing. Fish in these streams usually run smaller than those found in deep, cold lakes but there's enough fast action to test young skill.

Chapter 2

How to catch fish

Methods, baits, lures, and equipment

Fortunately, it isn't necessary to be an expert angler to catch fish. If this was the case, many fishermen might just as well stay home. Some anglers, of course, are more skilled than others, but fish can be caught on hook and line by anyone with the right tackle, a basic understanding of fish habits, and a little patience.

No doubt most species of fresh-water fishes could be taken with nothing more than a cane pole, line, hook, and a lure or bait. However, most anglers fish for sport and relaxation as well as for food. Modern tackle is designed to produce maximum angling enjoyment and increase the number of fish landed.

The amount and variety of fishing tackle available today may be confusing to a beginning fisherman. While it is true that some tackle may appeal more to the anglers than to the fish, the majority of equipment has a specific purpose. It pays to buy good-quality fishing tackle made by a reputable manufacturer. This tackle, if cared for, will last for many years; but obviously, even quality equipment won't guarantee limit catches of fish. It's up to the fisherman to use his tackle effectively and correctly.

Experimentation is the best way to determine what kind of tackle and techniques are most successful in a particular part of the country. Every fisherman soon has his favorite lures, baits, rods, reels, and methods for catching fish. Selecting the tackle is part of the fun of fishing; using it skillfully increases his appreciation of the angling sport.

← A bit distasteful, but if worms are what fish want, that's what they will get!

Hooking natural baits

Minnows

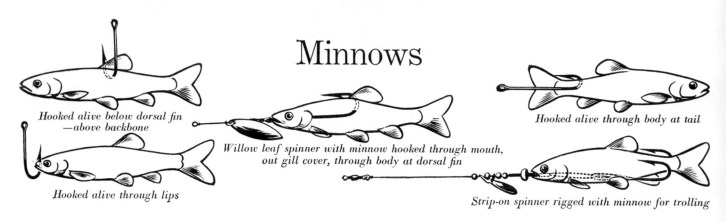

*Hooked alive below dorsal fin
—above backbone*

*Willow leaf spinner with minnow hooked through mouth,
out gill cover, through body at dorsal fin*

Hooked alive through body at tail

Hooked alive through lips

Strip-on spinner rigged with minnow for trolling

Frogs

Hooked alive through lips

Hooked alive through thigh

Double-hooked dead for casting or still fishing

Crayfish

Hooked dead through body

Live hooked through tail

Hard-shelled crayfish hooked through back

Hellgrammites White grubs

Worms

Grasshoppers Crickets

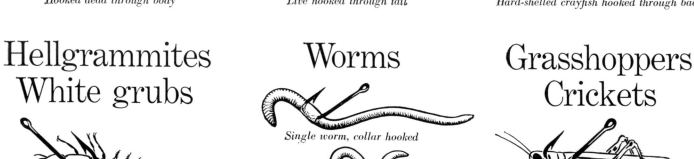

Hooked alive under hard collar

Single worm, collar hooked

Hooked through thorax

Grubs hooked just behind head

Single worm, looped along shank, barb buried

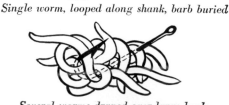

Several worms draped over large hook

Hooked dead through body

Basic tackle

Hooks

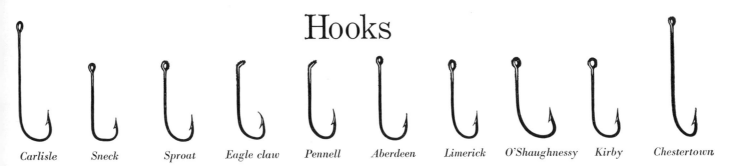

Carlisle   *Sneck*   *Sproat*   *Eagle claw*   *Pennell*   *Aberdeen*   *Limerick*   *O'Shaughnessy*   *Kirby*   *Chestertown*

Sinkers

Dipsey swivel sinker
has eyed shaft that swivels   *Bank sinker*   *Keel sinker*
prevents twisted line in trolling   *Slip sinkers — lead with*
hole in center slips on line   *Split shot*
crimped on line

Spindle sinker; lead ears   *Spindle sinker; rubber ears*   *Spindle sinker; swivel and snap*   *Lead tape; wrapped around line*

Bobbers

Real porcupine quill bobber — for light bait

Plastic bobber   *Pingpong ball; adhesive tape*   *Plastic quill bobber — for small fish*   *Cork bobber*

Spinners

Colorado spinner   *Abu-reflex spinner*

June bug spinner   *Mepps spinner*   *Spider spin spinner*

Hook ups

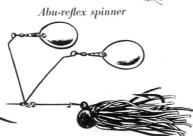

Popper bug with dropper
wet fly for bluegills

Drop sinker with
second leader above
holding bait off bottom

String of spinners for
trout and salmon called
"cow bells"

Artificial lures

Manufacturers have developed an extensive variety of fishing lures for every fish and every kind of fishing. The origin of the artificial lure likely started from these types of historical fishing experiences.

For centuries Eskimos carved fish lures of ivory, notching the front to give the lure proper action. In recent history, a story goes that once when a whittled wood piece was thrown into a stream, a bass struck at it. From this incident came the name "plug." A tablespoon, dropping over the side of a boat, made a wobbling motion in the water, causing a fish to rush at it. The clever angler cut off the spoon handle, attached a hook to the bowl, and thus developed the type of lure called a spoon.

Fishing lures constantly change in style. Shown here are a few popular ones among the extensive variety. Each area requires special lures to meet its fishing needs. Wise anglers seek advice of local fishermen and try their favorites.

Swivels, snaps and leaders

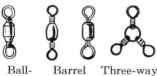

Ball-bearing swivel   Barrel swivels   Three-way swivel   Snap and swivel

Swivels and snaps. It pays to buy the best of these items. A line is no stronger than the snap; a poor swivel can cause twists and snarls.

Leaders, widely used with braided lines, can often be omitted with monofilament lines. Some anglers, however, use a steel leader when angling for fish with sharp teeth.

One of many types of leaders rigged for a spinner and hooks.

Nylon-coated steel leader with barrel swivel and snap attached. Comes in various lengths.

Nylon-coated steel leader with a ball-bearing swivel and snap. Length ranges from 6 to 24 inches.

Surface lures

These lures will generally remain on or near the surface, creating a disturbance in the water as they are retrieved. Some pop, bubble and gurgle due to a scooped out head. Others wobble and splash, using external flippers and collars. The angler should let the plug rest a moment after the cast, then give it a twitch or two before a slow, erratic retrieve.

Subsurface lures

Some of these plugs will remain on the surface until they are pulled under during the retrieve. The faster they are retrieved, the deeper some go. Others sink upon hitting the water and rise only when retrieved. Weights can be used with most lures to get them deeper in summer. A good trick when trolling is to let out a lot of line so the lure will sink deeper. Plugs come in a variety of sizes and colors.

Spoons & wobblers

Many times spoons will outstrip natural baits in numbers of fish caught. But be sure to use good swivels with spoons or these lures will twist the line with their action. Spoons generally sink swiftly so pick up the retrieve, in weedy or rocky lakes before they hang up on the bottom. Some spoons have weedless guards to help around snags and rushes. New spoons are available with retractable hooks.

Bottom bouncers

Eels and worms used singly or with jigs and spinner rigs are becoming popular. Many soft plastic models show a remarkable likeness to the natural baits.

Jigs come in a variety of weights and shapes utilizing bucktail, hair, and marabou. They are effective lures.

Plastics include soft imitation baits. They have received recent acceptance among natural bait fishermen and have won many anglers to artificial lures.

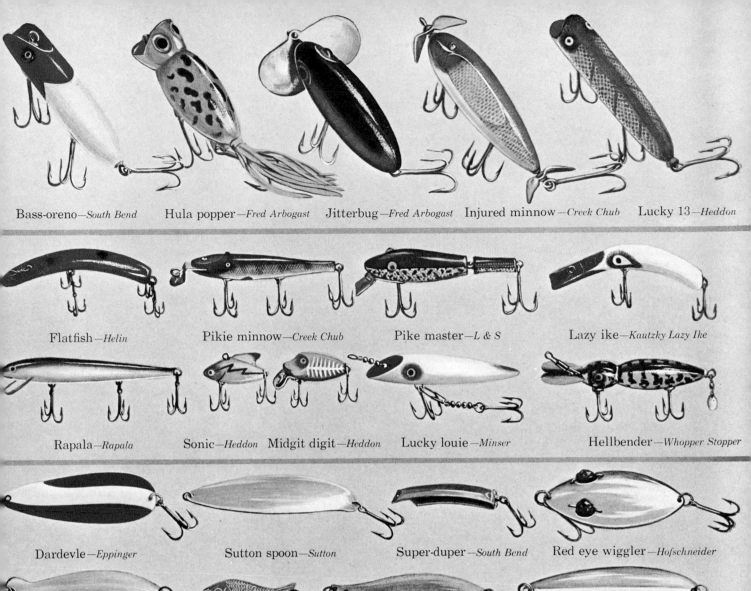

Bass-oreno—*South Bend*   Hula popper—*Fred Arbogast*   Jitterbug—*Fred Arbogast*   Injured minnow—*Creek Chub*   Lucky 13—*Heddon*

Flatfish—*Helin*   Pikie minnow—*Creek Chub*   Pike master—*L & S*   Lazy ike—*Kautzky Lazy Ike*

Rapala—*Rapala*   Sonic—*Heddon*   Midgit digit—*Heddon*   Lucky louie—*Minser*   Hellbender—*Whopper Stopper*

Dardevle—*Eppinger*   Sutton spoon—*Sutton*   Super-duper—*South Bend*   Red eye wiggler—*Hofschneider*

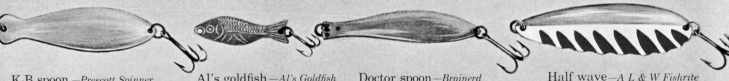

K-B spoon—*Prescott Spinner*   Al's goldfish—*Al's Goldfish*   Doctor spoon—*Brainerd*   Half wave—*A L & W Fishrite*

on's silver minnow—*Louis Johnson*   Pork rind—*Lutz*

Eel pork rind
Louis Johnson

Bass-buster—*Bass-Buster Lures*   Glit-r-jig fly—*Al Nelson*   Tadpole—*DeLong*

Doll-fly—*Thompson*   Upperman bucktail—*Bill Upperman*   Crayfish—*Creme Lure*

Wigly jig crawler
Kautzky Lazy Ike   Canadian jig fly—*Mille Lacs*   Rock-a-roo—*Cap's Tackle*   Lil' bass—*Fred Arbogast*

Maynard Reece

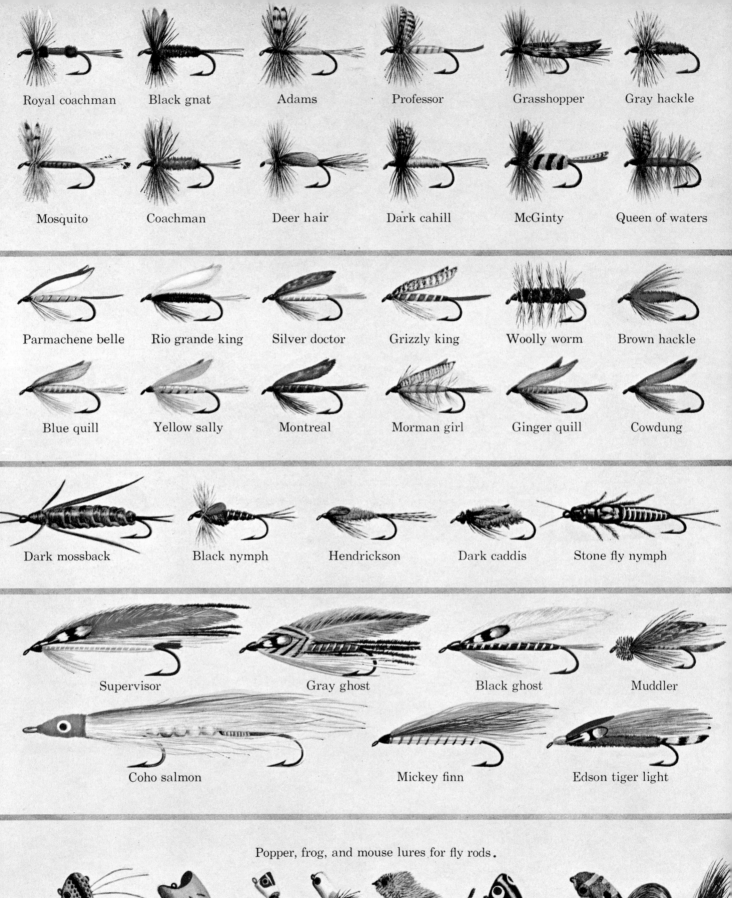

Royal coachman	Black gnat	Adams	Professor	Grasshopper	Gray hackle
Mosquito	Coachman	Deer hair	Dark cahill	McGinty	Queen of waters

Parmachene belle	Rio grande king	Silver doctor	Grizzly king	Woolly worm	Brown hackle
Blue quill	Yellow sally	Montreal	Morman girl	Ginger quill	Cowdung

Dark mossback	Black nymph	Hendrickson	Dark caddis	Stone fly nymph

Supervisor	Gray ghost	Black ghost	Muddler
Coho salmon		Mickey finn	Edson tiger light

Popper, frog, and mouse lures for fly rods.

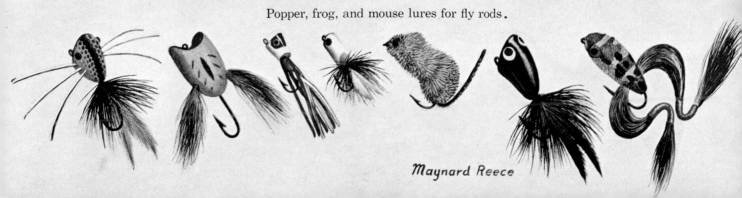

Maynard Reece

Dry flies

The controversial dry fly is designed to float and to make a fish strike. Beyond that, many arguments arise. One group favors flies that are easy for the angler to see in different light and water. Others concentrate on duplicating insects. Fish dry flies up- or across-stream stripping in line as it floats toward you. Fishing downstream may drown the fly.

Wet flies

Wet flies are fished at various depths, sometimes on the bottom. Some of these popular patterns can be tied wet or dry. Cast across stream, allowing the fly to sink and drift. When downstream and line is straight, jerk the fly with rod tip several times, each time letting fly drift back. Retrieve line by erratic jerks.

Nymphs

These flies attempt to imitate the larval stages of insects. They are usually fished similar to technique used for wet flies.

Streamers and bucktails

These flies imitate minnows or small food fish, both in color or shape and method they are presented. Fish streamers and bucktails similar to wet flies, retrieving them in short pulls, letting them drift back downstream often. To make these flies appear alive and darting takes practice, but is worth the effort.

Surface lures

On fly rods these tiny surface lures are deadly for bluegills and other members of the sunfish family. Cast over feeding grounds or spawning beds in the evening or early morning letting the lure sit a moment, then twitching it once or twice before retrieving slowly. The possibility of attracting a large bass or northern increases the suspense of such sport.

Flies and poppers

Flies are used primarily in fishing for the salmon, trout, grayling, and whitefish family. They are also productive for other species of fishes, particularly the sunfish family, as are small popper and surface frog lures.

Knots

Nylon-monofilament lines and leaders require special knots if they are to hold and retain full strength. Anglers should be certain to pull each knot tight, slowly and evenly, and to put at least five turns around any standing line.

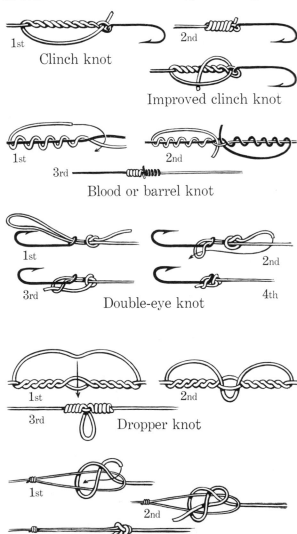

1st 2nd Clinch knot

Improved clinch knot

1st 2nd 3rd Blood or barrel knot

1st 2nd 3rd 4th Double-eye knot

1st 2nd 3rd Dropper knot

1st 2nd 3rd Tucked sheet bend knot

Still fishing

Still fishing is not only the most relaxing way to fish, but it's also a good method for catching certain species of sport fish. This technique is just what its name implies. The angler sits and waits for the fish to come to his bait or lure.

This method of fishing is most often used for perch, catfish, bullhead, panfish, and freshwater drum. However, almost every species of fish is a likely candidate for the still fisherman's hook.

Tackle for still fishing can be simple and inexpensive. Cane poles, spinning rods, fly rods, and casting rods are all used successfully. Some fishermen, and a great many youngsters, use nothing more than a hook and a piece of fish line held in their hands.

Many kinds of bait and a variety of artificial lures adapt to still fishing. Worms, minnows, crayfish, frogs, grasshoppers, crickets, salmon eggs, and many concoctions of dough baits are frequent choices. Spinners or jigs are artificial lures commonly used alone or with several combinations of natural and soft plastic baits.

Many still fisherman use a float or bobber attached above the bait to tell when a fish is biting. When the float begins to bob or goes under the surface the fisherman knows he has a bite. The bobber is also useful for holding the bait at the desired depth.

A bobber is ideal for the very young fisherman without much experience because it gives visible evidence of a fish biting. When a float isn't used, still fishermen either keep a finger on the line or watch the rod or pole tip for evidence of a biting fish.

Anglers should check their bait often when still fishing. Some species of fish are experts at stealing bait without the fisherman being aware of it. Many still fishermen move the bait up and down slowly to give it some movement which may attract a passing fish. When spinnerbait combinations or jigs are used, a vertical rather than a horizontal movement is necessary to get desired action from the lure.

Fishing through ice

Short rods are best for ice fishing. A reel may be attached, but in shallow water the line ties directly to the rod. When the fish hits, the angler raises the rod straight up, lifting fish through the hole in ice.

Some fishermen cut several holes in the ice and drop a bait in each, propping rods up so all can be watched. Caution: States often limit the number of rods an angler can use.

A relaxing morning

A boat, spinning tackle, and hungry bluegills make a perfect combination for young fishermen. Few outdoor sports can hold the interest of youngsters longer than fishing.

These anglers are using worms, a favorite bait for the scrappy bluegill. Long spinning rods allow them to cover more area. Life jackets are essential for youngsters in a boat.

Fishing from a dock

← Dock fishing is a relaxed method of catching fish as evidenced by this young angler and his father still fishing for crappies using minnows for bait.

Many species of fish congregate around boat docks, pilings, and rock piles. Such places provide good hiding and feeding areas. Some fish move into such areas in the evening and feed during the night, returning to deeper water during the warm part of the day. Others remain there day and night.

Trolling

Trolling is an effective way to take many species of fish. For some fish, at certain seasons of the year, it is the only method that produces consistent results.

Trolling means pulling a lure behind an oar- or motor-driven boat. Trolling behind a motor-driven boat is forbidden in some areas; it's best to check state laws before fishing.

Advantages of trolling for fish

By trolling, the fisherman can cover a wide area in a short period. When fishing in unknown waters, trolling is the fastest method of learning where fish are located. Trolling also appeals to many fishermen because it is a relaxing way to fish. The angler simply holds the rod and waits for a fish to hit the lure. The fisherman has time to enjoy the beauty of the surrounding area while his tackle is doing the work.

When several anglers are in one boat, trolling is often a practical method of fishing. Bait casting or spinning is difficult when in close quarters and flying hooks can be outright dangerous if not cast with great care.

Techniques and equipment

Usually, lures should be trolled slowly, though just how slowly is impossible to state. At times, fish will hit fairly fast-moving lures when they won't pay any attention to slow moving rigs. The best advice is for an angler to try trolling at different speeds until he begins to catch fish, then stick to that speed.

If someone is rowing the boat while the angler trolls, it usually is best for the angler to sit in the stern and face the person rowing. If trolling from a motor-driven boat, with someone operating the motor, the fisherman should sit facing the stern so he can watch his line, keeping it free of the motor.

Rods for trolling should be fairly stiff, yet have enough spring to help in fighting the fish. Glass or metal rods are fine for trolling. A good bait-casting rod is usually adequate for this method of fishing.

When the lure must be trolled at great depth, a very stiff rod is needed to comfortably handle the combined weight of line, lure, and fish. Met-al lines often are used for fishing deep water.

Deep trolling for lake trout or landlocked salmon requires a stiff rod and usually a line of copper wire, braided wire, Monel metal, or a line with a metal core. If you use a braided nylon line for deep trolling, use swivels to connect the lure to the line.

Lures used for trolling usually are of three types; spoons, subsurface lures, or spinners. Many variations of spoons and wobblers are available in copper, nickel, and brass finishes or in a combination of finishes. Spoons with painted colors are popular—a combination of red and white is a proven fish-getter. Subsurface lures will go below the surface when trolled. Some will run deep but others need to be weighted for certain trolling conditions.

Spinners make versatile trolling lures that troll with or without bait on the hook. Fishermen trolling with spinners often use minnows or other small species of bait fish. Some spinners have colored feathers or a bucktail to hide their treble hooks. These are effective for muskellunge, northern pike, smallmouth bass.

Always use swivels when trolling with spoons or spinners to prevent line twists. When fishing for species that have sharp teeth, use a wire or nylon-coated wire leader between line, lure.

Lures must be trolled effectively

With a little experience, most anglers get the "feel" of trolled lures. It is not difficult to tell when a lure is working properly. Spoons and spinners send a steady beat to the rod. Any time the beat stops, the lure should be retrieved and checked for weeds, locked swivels, or fouled hooks.

Fishermen often augment the natural action of a trolled lure to entice fish to hit. They speed up and slow down the lure by slowly raising and lowering the rod tip. Jerking the rod gives the lure a fast, darting action.

When a fish hits a trolled lure, stop the boat at once and play him as though he had been caught while casting. If a motor-driven boat is not stopped, the fish may drown from being dragged through the water. Also, the additional pressure of the water might break the line or tear the hook out of the fish's mouth.

These anglers are trolling for lake trout in Great Bear Lake near Arctic Circle →

An accurate cast to the edge of weeds brought this lunker bass out of hiding

The ability to cast a lure with accuracy is not only satisfying to a fisherman's ego, but it also will result in more fish caught. The bait-casting rod should not be less than 5 feet in length. Shorter rods will usually be too stiff for accurate casting and for enjoying the fighting ability of the fish. Metal, glass, and bamboo bait-casting rods are available in a range of lengths and degrees of stiffness for all types of fishing.

Bait casting

Because bait- and plug-casting equipment is accurate and simple to use it is the favorite of many fishermen. Accurate casting is especially important when fishing for bass, northern pike, or other species of fish found in small openings in weed beds or next to submerged logs or rocks.

The correct method of using bait-casting tackle is not difficult to learn, but proficiency takes practice. Begin by grasping the rod handle with your casting hand and turning the rod until the reel handle is straight up and the reel spool is to the left.

Place your thumb on the reel spool to prevent the line from running out, then bring the rod up until the tip is a little above horizontal. Point the rod at the spot you want the plug to hit. The plug should be 5 inches or less from the rod tip at this point. Swing the rod up and back to a spot a little behind your shoulder and with your casting hand at eye level or above, bring the rod forward sharply. At the same time, reduce the pressure of your thumb on the spool, allowing the plug to carry the line out. Keep your thumb in light contact with the spool as the line is running out. When your bait or plug has nearly reached the spot you are aiming for, begin to brake the spool with your thumb.

The instant the plug hits the water, clamp down on the spool with your thumb. If you don't you will end up with a backlash caused when the reel spool is turning faster than the outgoing line. As soon as the spool has been stopped, shift the rod to your other hand and grasp the reel handle with your casting hand. You are now ready for business!

Many anglers practice bait casting in their back yards. An old tire makes a good target. When practicing, keep in mind that accuracy is usually more important than distance. It is a good idea to become accurate at distances of less than 50 feet before attempting long casts.

The newest types of reels incorporate some of the refinements of spinning reels and the star-drag brake from salt-water tackle. As you are about to cast, a button disconnects the spool from the reel handle permitting the line to play off a free spool. The star-drag brake takes over on retrieve to help play the fish. When pressure is exerted on the tackle, the drag gives line rather than allowing the fish to break free.

Quality tackle was required to stand the fight put up by this prize lake trout caught in Great Bear Lake near the Arctic Circle. The angler (above) keeps a tight line on his tired fish while a guide leans over the boat with net. The reel's star-drag brake helps to keep the line tight, yet permits give if the fish should decide to make another run and exerts force on line.

Fishing for trout in mountain stream

One of the great thrills in fishing is the leap of a trout after a dry fly. This successful fisherman is handling his fly rod well, keeping the tip high and forcing the fish to fight the spring. The line is usually retrieved by hand and allowed to float on the water until the fish is landed. Or, with an automatic reel the line can be wound as it is retrieved.

Opening day of trout season

← In some areas, especially in the eastern part of the United States, crowds of fly fishermen take to the streams on opening day of the trout season. Many streams are stocked with hatchery-reared trout prior to opening day. In this situation, many anglers use shorter fly rods which offer better control and result in fewer flies snagged in trees, brush, or people.

Solitary fishing on a Canadian river

Those who think fly fishing is strictly a man's sport → better look again at this addition to the scenery. Women can not only gain unusual skill with the fly rod, but have the patience needed to delicately drop a fly to the proper spot below a rock on a swift moving river. And their nimble fingers can tie a dry fly, nymph, or streamer to fool any trout.

Fly casting

Fly fishing for certain species of fish provides maximum angling enjoyment. This is probably the most difficult of all casting methods to learn though it can be mastered by any fisherman with co-ordination and patience to practice.

Fly rods made from split bamboo or fiberglass come in a variety of lengths and weights. For beginners, a rod about 7½ feet in length and weighing 4 to 5 ounces is a good choice. The fly rod reel, either conventional or automatic winding, is the least important of any type of fishing reel. Many anglers, however, use the reel for playing the fish.

To practice fly casting, first tie a 5-foot piece of nylon leader to the line. Grip the handle of the rod with your thumb extended along the top of the handle so the reel is beneath the rod. Pull 15 or more feet of line from the reel straight out in front of you. Hold the line with the left hand, ahead and to the side of the reel.

To begin the cast, bring the rod tip up slowly, increasing the speed until the rod reaches a point a little past vertical. The elbow reaches shoulder height, with the forearm providing the upward lift and the wrist accenting the whip action of the rod. Pause as the rod reaches the one o'clock position to give the line time to straighten out behind you.

As you feel a slight pull on the rod tip, begin the forward cast. Start forward and increase the speed until the forearm is parallel with the water. At this point the rod will be in a slight upward position. Lower the rod slowly until it is parallel with the water and the line and fly will land gently. These basic steps are repeated with constant rhythm as you work out more line.

Spinning

Spinning tackle is a relative newcomer to North American fishermen. Introduced in the 1930s, it has gained acceptance from both novice and veteran for its simplicity of operation and its versatility.

An important advantage of spinning tackle is the elimination of the backlash problem. A spinning reel has a stationary spool. The line strips off the end of the spool rather than unwinding from a revolving spool.

Another advantage is that spinning tackle enables an angler to cast very light lures long distances. Lightweight monofilament or braided lines, plus the elimination of a revolving spool reduces the drag on the line so light lures and baits can be cast much farther than with bait- or fly-casting tackle.

There are a number of different types of spinning reels. The open-face reel with the spool of line exposed is available with either manual or automatic line pickup. The closed-face spinning reel has the spool covered by a metal shell and the line is automatically picked up by the spool after the cast. Both of these reels are mounted on the underside of the spinning rod.

The spin-casting reel has a closed face and is used in the same manner as the bait-casting reel. This reel sits on top of the rod during the cast and has a thumb level which controls the speed of the outgoing line.

Spinning rods are usually longer and more flexible than those used for bait casting. Most spinning-tackle fishermen use a 6 to 7 foot rod made of metal, glass, or bamboo.

Spinning tackle is easy to use

After a little practice almost anyone can make consistently long casts using a spinning reel. It is more difficult, however, to make accurate casts with this tackle than with bait-casting equipment. The fixed spool eliminates the precise thumb control of the line possible with bait-casting tackle though some finger control is possible with the open-face type of spinning reel. Casting with the spin-cast reel requires a technique similar to that used with a bait-casting reel.

When using an open-face spinning reel, begin your cast by gripping the rod with the reel stem between the second and third fingers and the thumb on top of the rod handle. The line should be held between the index finger and the rod handle. When ready to cast, use your left hand to push the line-holding bail out of the way so the line can run freely off the spool.

Point the rod at the target and bring it up sharply to a position a little past vertical. As soon as the weight of the lure has bent the rod tip backward, bring the rod forward in a continuous motion, at the same time releasing the line held with the index finger. As the lure nears the spot you are aiming at, slow it down by brushing your index finger against the line near the tip of the reel spool. Beginners usually make the mistake of releasing the line too soon when the rod is brought forward which results in the lure shooting straight up in the air.

Spinning reels have a brake which can be set to control the amount of tension on the line as a fish is reeled in. If a fish exerts more pull on the line than the brake is set for, the fish takes out line even though the angler continues to turn the reel handle. The brake tension is often adjusted while playing the fish. Some reels attain less tension by reversing the reel handle a partial turn; forward turn restores tension.

Ready for fish to strike

Children can easily handle light spinning tackle. This young lady is using an open-face spinning reel and small lure for trout fishing in a western lake.

One of the easiest ways to cast a fly or light lure with spinning equipment is to use a small plastic ball partially filled with water to give it weight; a short leader connects ball and fly. This ball will float like a bobber yet has no adverse effect on most fish. Completely filling the ball with water causes it to sink just below the surface while keeping the wet fly suspended free from snagging in the rocks as it might with a sinker.

Two-handed casting

His casting form may be unorthodox, but with a closed-face spincast reel this young fisherman does not have to worry about a backlash. Children and some women do not have the power in one wrist to get a long cast, so it is quite natural with spinning tackle to use the two-handed heave, similar to the method used by salt-water surf fishermen.

This method is a more sensible solution than to force a child to use only one arm and then see a good rod and reel sail out of a tiny hand into deep water. Youngsters aren't interested in a casting exhibition, but just want to catch fish.

Steady pressure on fish

 One advantage of spinning tackle is the ability for novices and experts alike to keep a tight line for close-in fighting of fish. A sudden surge under the boat can allow the fish enough slack to snap the line, but with spinning tackle, constant drag keeps the line taut.

Playing and netting the fish

Once the big job of getting a fish to take a lure or bait is accomplished, the wise angler plays his prize slow and easy. After all, the fun is in the battle, so why hurry to end it?

When a fish strikes, quickly set the hooks by raring back with the rod tip. Then reel rapidly to keep a tight line in case your initial jerk causes any slack. Normally, as soon as a fish is hooked, he will make a short run which can be met by keeping the rod tip high and not reeling but maintaining pressure.

Veteran anglers always keep a bend in their rods, by keeping the rod tip up. This forces the fish to fight the constant pressure of the rod which eventually tires him to the point where he can be netted safely.

Once the fish begins a run, give line only to prevent the line from breaking or if you think the tension may pull the hook from the fish's mouth. With spinning or spin-casting tackle, of course, the fish will take line despite your cranking whenever the pull is stronger than the tension set on the reel.

If the fish can be kept below the surface, so much the better. There he must fight not only the line tension, but the water pressure as well. On top, the fish has a better chance of tearing the hook loose. When a fish comes to the surface and leaps, slackening the tension on the line will often send him diving to the bottom.

Be sure to completely exhaust your opponent before landing him. Even large fish are easily boated if they are thoroughly tired first. Don't run the chance of losing your fish by hurrying.

When a fish is lively and diving like this pike, most anglers keep him away from the boat until he's worn out.

How not to land a battling fish

This angler is about to lose a prize catch in his eagerness to get the fish in the boat. In heavily fished waters this is heart-breaking. Of course, with a strong rod and high-test line, almost any fish can be horsed in if the hook doesn't pull out. But the sport in fishing comes with skillful use of the lightest equipment needed for a particular species.

Obviously this angler hasn't played the fish long enough to take the fight out of him. As a result, the fish is too fresh for the net man to do more than excite the fish and help him throw the hook.

Unless extremely tired, most fish will make a final, desperate run for freedom as soon as they sight the angler or the boat. With the fish so close to the rod tip, little of the rod's action can be used to absorb the tension on the line and the resulting pressure can either break the line or tear the hook from the fish.

A tired fish ready for the net

This angler was in no hurry to bring his catch to the boat. He played the fish away from the boat until it turned side-up in the water. Most fish, when tired, will come to the surface and turn on their side. This is the time to quickly bring him to the netting position before he recovers.

Lower the net into the water before the fish is close to the boat, then lead him into the net head first, and quickly raise the net with the fish inside. Inexperienced fishermen in a hurry to boat their fish often try netting their prize tail first. This can result in frightening the fish into a final run out of the net and off the line.

An angler should keep tension on the line once the fish is in the net to prevent the lure from becoming entangled and causing needless work.

More than one way to land a fish

Fishermen who prefer to net their catch should be certain the opening is wide enough and the net is deep enough to retain the fish. Though netting is perhaps the easiest and most popular way of landing a fish, several other techniques are common.

A gaff is used by some fishermen, usually for the larger species of fish. If the fish is to be released the angler should slip the point of the gaff carefully into the body at the gill cavity, then lift the fish smoothly into the boat.

Some fish can be landed by hand. Grip the lower jaw firmly with thumb in his mouth, forefinger on outside and lift smoothly. Another method is to press thumb and finger into his eye sockets, lifting the fish by his bone structure. Both methods paralyze the fish momentarily, but do not injure him. The mouth grip works best on fish without teeth. Be careful of hooks.

Chain stringer with safety-pin holder inserted through softer spots of both jaws prevents this pike from escaping.

Keeping the fish

Fish always taste better if they are dressed as soon as possible after they're taken from the water. Most fishermen don't want to take the time to dress each fish as it is caught; the next best solution is to keep it alive.

Keeping captive fish alive can be done in a number of ways. For small fish, a burlap sack or a net of heavy cord hung over the side of the boat is ideal for this purpose. Or a 5-gallon pail partially filled with water will ride in the bottom of the boat; the water should be changed every half hour to keep the fish alive.

Use a heavy cord stringer for medium to large species without teeth. Large fish with teeth require a chain stringer with large safety-pin-type holders. For any type of stringer insert the pin or cord through the softer part of both the upper and lower jaws of the fish.

Always lift a stringer or net of fish into the boat before moving to another place on the lake. Fish can live on a stringer pulled slowly through the water, but they will drown at the higher speeds of motor-driven boats.

It's unhandy to place fish on a stringer when fishing a stream where an angler moves often. In such cases a canvas creel, which has some insulating properties, or a wicker creel is the choice of most fishermen. Wet grass placed in the bottom of the creel will help keep the fish cool. Fish kept in such manner will definitely stay cooler much longer than those thrown on the ground or left to spoil in the sun.

Panfish

Pail

Fish bag

Trout

Basket creel

Canvas creel

Releasing the fish

Many fish taken by anglers are released as soon as they are caught. The fish may be too small, out of season, or the angler may have all the fish he requires for his table but doesn't want to stop fishing. Whenever a sport fish isn't wanted, for any reason, it should be returned to the water.

Removing a hook from the mouth of a fish by jerking it with a pair of pliers and then "throwing" the fish back into the water is not the practice of a good sportsman. Such treatment can impair the fish's ability to feed, can even cause internal injuries resulting in the death of the fish, leaving it to float on the surface a short time later.

With few exceptions, a fish out of water is a delicate living thing. If it is to be released, it should be treated as gently as possible. Probably the best method of releasing an unwanted fish is to cut the hook as close to the fish's mouth as possible without removing the fish from the water. A pair of fisherman's pliers will cut the hook easily. Most fish released in this manner will live.

If the hook is inside the fish's mouth, cut the leader. Fish will usually manage to disengage a hook once they are free of the line. If not, many fish get along fine with the hook attached to their jaw.

If an angler doesn't want to, or can't cut the hook or leader, he can grasp the hook with a pair of pliers and hold it, shank down. The fish will often slide off the hook uninjured. If an angler must hold a fish with his hands to disengage the hook, he should always wet his hands first. Dry hands remove part of the protective mucus on some fish, especially the smooth-skinned species, and permit a fungus disease to attack the fish. After the fisherman wets his hands, he can grasp the fish's body lightly behind the gills. The fish should not be removed from the water if it can be avoided.

If a fish is removed from the water to disengage the hook, the fish will often be unable to remain upright when returned. A fisherman can often help the fish recover by holding it lightly and moving it slowly backward and forward in the water. The action forces water through the gills, stimulating the fish's breathing action, and generally he will soon swim away.

This northern pike, carefully unhooked and released in the water, will live to provide future angling thrills.

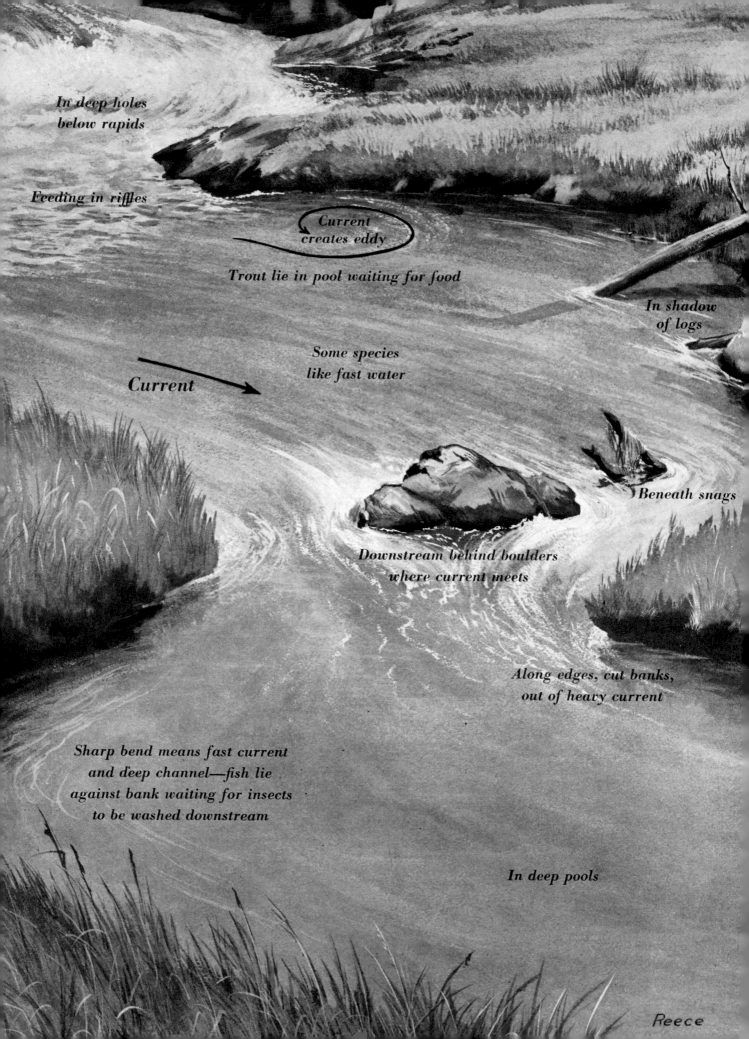

Chapter 3

Where to catch fish

Fish and their habits

Solving the problem of where to catch a particular species of fish makes angling an intriguing sport. If the fisherman knew exactly where each fish was hiding, the suspense of finding it and the satisfaction that comes with a successful catch would diminish considerably.

In this sport, it is common for an angler to chase across a lake after a lunker only to return home hours later and tie into one in front of his cabin.

Nevertheless, certain facts concerning the habits of various fish families remain constant. These facts help experienced anglers to be consistently able to work a lake or stream and produce fish. Knowing when and how to fish is certainly a big help, but knowing where to fish is even more important. The skillful angler cannot bring in fish if he is fishing in the wrong part of a stream or lake. Smart fishermen make a mental note when they catch each species to remember the habitat as a future guide.

Salmon and trout family

← Salmon and trout generally prefer similar spots in streams to hide, rest, or feed. At certain periods they will come to the surface to feed on insects, but usually they need to be enticed from hiding. Most species don't like to fight the fastest water; look for them behind rocks, snags, along undercut banks, or under overhanging tree boughs. Some like riffles or slick areas at the front or tail of currents. These fish are flighty so stalk them cautiously.

Pike family

Members of the pike family have enormous appetites; they are generally found in spots where they can hide and wait for forage fish, frogs, or crayfish. As pike are the most predatory of all the fishes, they will move into areas such as those below dams or up tributary streams where large numbers of small fish congregate.

Because they are always on the prowl, this is one family that is likely to strike your bait or lure any place on the lake.

Around logs and submerged trees

Outside of lily pads

In and around bulrushes and weed beds

Below rapids and waterfalls

Up small streams and channels connecting lakes

Reece

Along shallow weedy shorelines of bays and rivers

Catfish family

Catfish are primarily nocturnal feeders, so fishing is best during the early evening and night in the river channel. In the daytime they are found hiding in deep holes, under drift piles, below dams and impoundments, or in any heavily covered area.

The catfish family is sensitive to noise or disturbance; be quiet when you approach a catfish hole. If they are frightened by an angler's threshing about, there will be no fishing.

In caves undercut along bank

In deep holes cut out by current

Inside hollow submerged logs

Around log and driftwood piles

In channel at night—below sand bars on drop offs during feeding periods

Bass family
White bass, yellow bass, striped bass

The true basses are most prevalent in the reservoirs or impoundments of the eastern and southern United States. A favorite method of finding white bass is to fish "the jumps" or to watch for signs of fish churning the surface after minnows. By racing to the spot most anglers are able to find productive fishing for a short time. Then the fish move on and repeat the performance in another spot. Striped bass are fished deep. Their habits are erratic. Most bass will feed in shallow water in early spring and in the evenings, but stay deep in cooler water during hot days. They move in schools; concentrate fishing in one spot once you find them.

Migrate up flooded, swollen streams and rivers to spawn in spring

Schooling fish churn water surface chasing minnows, alerting fishermen

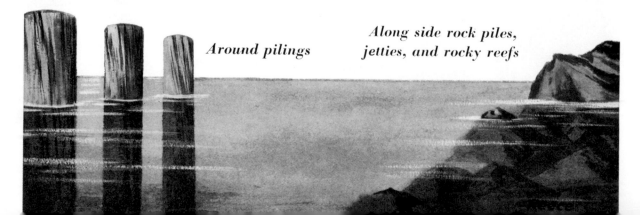

Around pilings

Along side rock piles, jetties, and rocky reefs

Perch family
Walleye, sauger, yellow perch

Like the bass family the walleye, sauger, and yellow perch are schooling fish. Work their various habitats. Once you find them, confine your fishing to that area until the school moves on. Walleyes will move up small streams, channels, and inlets in early spring to spawn; hit these first. As the season progresses, keep working toward the main lake and into deeper water. At night, they move into the shallows to feed. Both walleyes and saugers like to stay and feed below dams or deep holes in rivers. Yellow perch feed in the daytime, preferring submerged weed beds or shaded spots under docks where they can hide from their enemies.

In narrow channels and inlets early in spring

Along rocky shore lines, deep drop offs

Near rocky reefs both above and below surface

Around islands

Over underwater sand bars

Among submerged weed beds for yellow perch

Along shallow beaches at night

Reece

Sunfish family
Largemouth bass

Largemouths prefer habitats similar to pike except in tighter, more confined spaces such as under weeds, logs, or brush. Often they feed so close to shore that their backs stick out of the water. These bass like to hide around stumps and brush. In reservoirs or impoundments they're found near submerged trees or next to steep hills that cut sharply into the water.

Close to shore

Around logs, submerged sticks, stumps

At tip of points

Among lily pads

Along weed beds

Smallmouth bass

This is a fish with habits quite different from those of the largemouth, preferring deep lakes of cold, clear water. Search for smallmouths against rocky shorelines, reefs, and in fast water between lakes and rapids. In rivers they will be found around gravel or rock riffles, deep rocky holes, or working where the current washes food down to them. They like cold spring water.

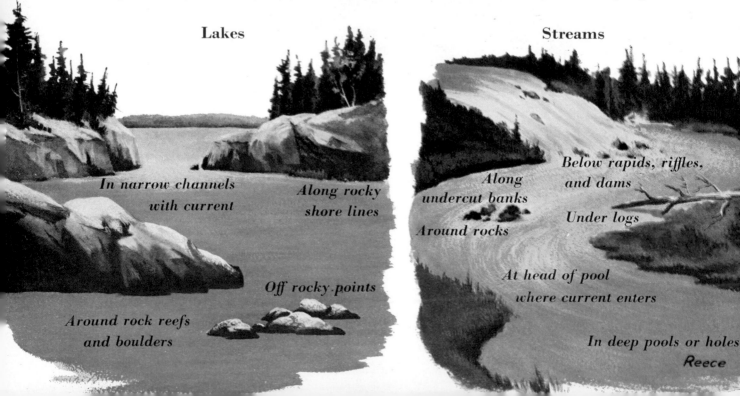

Lakes

Streams

In narrow channels with current

Along rocky shore lines

Off rocky points

Around rock reefs and boulders

Along undercut banks

Around rocks

Below rapids, riffles, and dams

Under logs

At head of pool where current enters

In deep pools or holes

Reece

Bluegills, sunfish, crappies

The panfish have a more limited habitat than other members of the sunfish family and therefore are easier to find. They will be in schools around weeds and nests in spawning season, or in deep holes during hot weather. Once you locate these productive areas, particularly the deeper holes, you can return for many years and expect consistently good results.

Around nests in spawning season

Feeding in shallow water in the evening

In shallow inlets and small weedy areas

Along cut banks and under overhanging boughs of trees

Under docks in shadow areas

Reece

Chapter 4

When to fish

Weather conditions

Calm days

To most fishermen, the answer to the question, "when to fish?" would be "any time the opportunity arises." The more time an angler spends fishing, in most instances, means the more fish he will catch. Nonetheless, there are many factors in addition to time spent fishing that influence his success. Weather is one of these factors, and one in which fishermen are always vitally concerned.

Calm days are the most pleasant for the fisherman to be out on a lake or fishing from the lake shore or in a stream. Fish that rise to the surface to feed on insects can be seen much easier on calm days and anglers can direct their casts to these rises.

Calm days present the fisherman with some problems as well as some advantages. In clear water the fish are much more likely to be frightened off by seeing the fisherman or his boat than when the surface is rippled by wind. This means the fisherman must be extra cautious in approaching the area he wants to fish.

If the angler is fishing from the bank of a stream or lake, he should stay back from the edge of the water as much as possible. It's a good idea to use a longer cast on calm days which puts that much more distance between himself and the fish and lessens the chances of being seen. When casting from a motor-driven boat, he should shut off the motor upon entering the fishing area and row while casting along the shore.

Fishing with surface plugs or dry flies on calm days requires special care. Create as little splash as possible with your plug or fly. After casting, wait until the circles caused by the lure hitting the water disappear before beginning your retrieve. This technique gives the fish more time to get over the scare caused by the splash.

← On calm days, the mirrorlike water surface requires special fishing techniques

Windy days

Wind may make casting and boat handling difficult, but it often results in good fishing. Certain kinds of fish bite better when the surface of the water is covered with waves.

Some fish, especially smaller species such as bluegills, may move into protected areas if the wave action becomes strong. At these times fishing is best on the lee side of land points or in protected inlets and coves. Often insects and food are blown off the trees and weeds by the wind, dropping into the water. Some species of fish will move in to shallow water to feed during this period.

Wave action also moves food to fish which feed near drop offs or sandy and rocky bars. Fish usually found directly above bars will often move to the lee side on windy days and wait for the wave action to move the food to them.

Allowing the boat to drift with the wind is an excellent way to slowly troll either live or artificial bait over the fishing spots. A bait or lure will travel approximately the same speed as the natural fish food and, as a result, chances of fooling the fish are improved. When casting, move upwind of the fishing area and let the boat drift broadside to the wind.

Storms

Fishing just before or during a storm often results in excellent catches for those anglers who don't mind getting a little wet or windblown. Icthyologists can't come up with proven reasons for this, but there's little doubt in many a veteran fisherman's mind that fish go on a feeding spree just before or during a storm.

It's possible that an approaching storm affects some fish the same as approaching night. Many fish do most of their feeding in the evening. It is also possible that wind and rain blow and wash extra food into the water, and fish quickly take advantage of the opportunity to feed. A heavy rain may change the temperature and level of the water; both affect the feeding habits of fish.

Whatever the reasons, the angler should not pass up an opportunity to fish just because the weather is stormy. Storms, or any other type of weather, aren't factors guaranteeing good fishing, but foul weather may provide that extra, mysterious something that results in fish increasing their feeding activity.

Good safety judgment is essential when fishing during storms. An open lake is no place to be when lightning or high wind is expected.

Windy day fishing locations

As wind will blow available food into the water or disturb food already in the water; fish will often change their feeding habits to fit the new conditions.

Head for shore, or fish and get wet?

These anglers move closer to shore as storm approaches. In a boat, lifejackets should be worn by children and nonswimmers; with safety cushions for all.

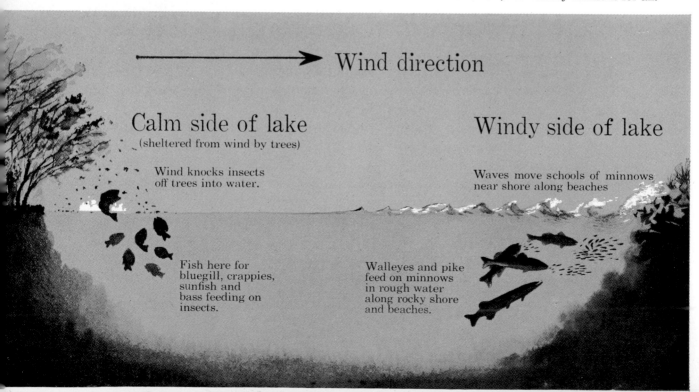

Wind direction

Calm side of lake
(sheltered from wind by trees)

Wind knocks insects off trees into water.

Fish here for bluegill, crappies, sunfish and bass feeding on insects.

Windy side of lake

Waves move schools of minnows near shore along beaches

Walleyes and pike feed on minnows in rough water along rocky shore and beaches.

Early hour, foggy weather encourages these bass anglers to try their skill at edge of lily pads or weed bed.

Time of day

The time of day an angler fishes varies in importance with each species of fish.

Some fish feed more at one time of the day than at another. Fish that feed primarily on insects are a good example. Because many insects hatch either early in the morning or late in the evening, it is during these periods that insect-eating fish are actively feeding.

Some trout fishermen mistakenly fish only early morning or in the evening, staying away from the water during the middle part of the day. However, many trout are caught in the middle of the day, so don't quit fishing just because the sun is high.

Other fish do much of their feeding in the evening or during the night. These fish move into shallow water in the evening in pursuit of small fish or other food, and spend much of the daylight hidden in deep water. Walleyes are a good example of evening and night feeders. But here again, many walleyes are caught in deeper holes during morning, noon, or afternoon hours.

Bass often move into shallow water in search of food in the morning and evening; bass fishing is often better during these hours than in any other part of the day. During the middle of the day, especially in warm weather, bass will seek the deep holes in a lake; fishing these spots can be very productive.

Water temperature has an important bearing on where fish are located. Many species of fish prefer a certain temperature range and will move into deep or shallow water until they find the most comfortable area. Cooler water during morning and evening attracts fish to shallows.

There have been widely accepted tables published to show major and minor fishing activity periods based on the moon and sun. However, most fishermen will do well to fish whenever they have the opportunity, regardless of the clock, bearing in mind that they can't catch fish without having their hooks in the water.

Evening fishermen move into shallower water in search of feeding walleyes →

Spring

This is the perfect time for catching many different species of fish. A fish's body temperature varies with the temperature of the water it swims in, so as the waters warm in spring most fish become more active; fighting characteristics improve. Fish will move into the shallower, warmer waters.

This is also the season when some species "school up" and move into the sun-warmed shallows to spawn, actively feeding during the process.

In many areas spring is simply a beautiful time of the year to fish when insects are less bothersome, days seem bright, air refreshing.

Summer

Most, but not all, species of fish seek the cooler, deeper areas of lakes, ponds, and rivers when the weather turns hot. In general, you will have to get your bait or lure down deep to reach most fish during the heat of the day and then you may not be successful. During the evening and early morning, fish often move into cooled shallow water to feed on small fish and insects.

Summer is the lazy, relaxing time to fish. Under a shelter of welcomed shade trees or on a quiet lake, with a rod in hand, it's easy to forget troubles and tensions and just dunk a worm or watch an artificial lure drift toward you.

Fall

Fishing success is usually greater when the weather begins to cool. Fish move from their deep, cool, summer hiding places into shallower water. For some species, feeding activity increases as the water temperature begins to drop and fishing is best just before the water freezes. This is a critical period of perhaps only a few days but the lucky fisherman who has the fish schedule accurate is in for a fast and productive trip full of thrills.

Whether you fly fish a stream for trout or still fish a lake for bullheads, fall is a choice time to be out of doors as nature prepares for winter.

Time of year

Winter

Numb fingers and toes are not uncommon in winter fishing but good catches of certain species are made at this time of year. Both open water and ice fishing are popular. Look for fish in the shallower water during winter months. Many western streams have migrating fish to encourage hardy steelhead fishermen.

At one time the fishing season ran only from late spring, through summer, and into early fall, then tackle was put away and sportsmen turned to other activities. Fortunately in North America today the situation has changed. Now there is an open season year around on certain species of fish and angling has become a full-time sport.

Increase in scientific knowledge regarding habitation, feeding, and reproduction is one important reason for legalizing year-around fishing on some species. Scientists learned that under-fishing is more harmful to many species than over-fishing.

The result of this fisheries research has been a reconsideration of fish conservation and a gradual liberalizing of fishing seasons with higher limits or, in some cases, no limits at all. This of course doesn't apply to all species of fish, but enough are included to keep most anglers busy throughout the year.

Nonetheless, the time of year an angler fishes does have an effect on the success of his venture. Some fish apparently have periods when feeding literally stops and fishing during this time is usually a waste of energy. Some species are almost impossible to catch once the water is frozen over, others continue active feeding throughout the winter. During the hot summer months certain species of fish stop feeding, and seek comfort in cool, deep holes, while some fish apparently feed all summer.

The fisherman today must be aware of influences each season of the year plays upon fish if he is to be consistently successful. It is not enough to know what bait or lure to use, unless he also understands how the seasonal influences have changed the fish's environment and influenced its habits.

Probably the greatest change in fishing regulations has been the increase in the number of fish which can be taken through the ice or from open water in winter months. Ice fishing and open-water winter fishing have grown rapidly in popularity, and in some parts of the country entire families take to the ice each weekend.

Usually, the species of fish which can be legally taken through the ice are those which tend to overpopulate a lake or stream, literally eating themselves out of existence. When ice fishing is allowed, and more of these fish are harvested, the overpopulation problem often decreases.

Structure & coloration

The color of a fish can be affected by age, spawning changes, habitat, and fading when the fish is removed from the water. Because it is so variable, color serves only as a partial help in identifying one species or family from another. Fortunately the physical characteristics remain more constant and offer a much better method of distinguishing the many kinds of fishes.

Some of these physical characteristics have been illustrated as an aid in helping the angler with the complex matter of identifying the exact fish he has caught. Since most fishermen lack equipment to disect their catch, only external features are shown for identification in the field.

Parts of a fish

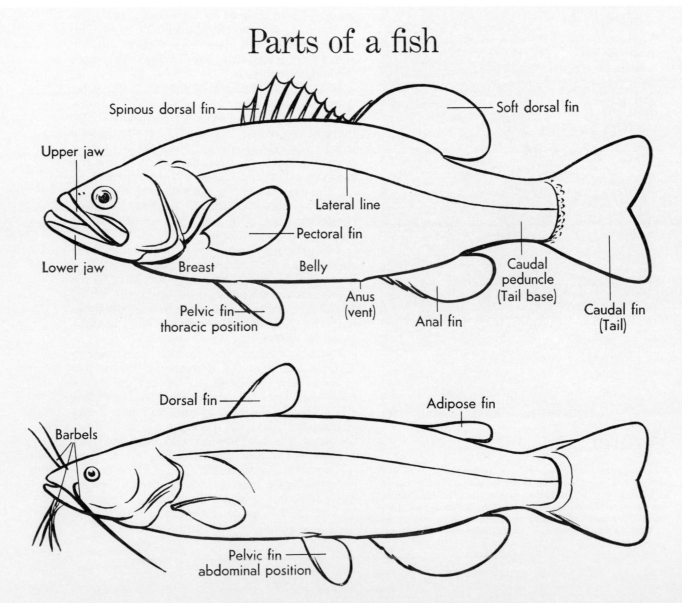

Chapter 5

How to identify fish

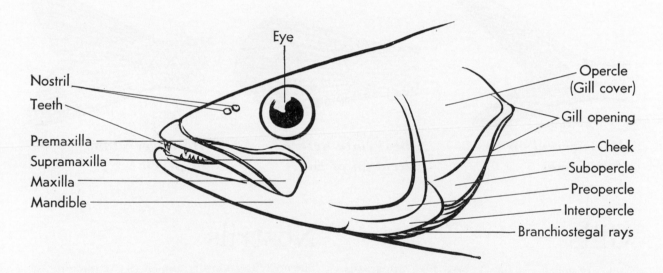

Eye

Nostril

Teeth

Premaxilla

Supramaxilla

Maxilla

Mandible

Opercle
(Gill cover)

Gill opening

Cheek

Subopercle

Preopercle

Interopercle

Branchiostegal rays

Methods of counting spines and rays on fins

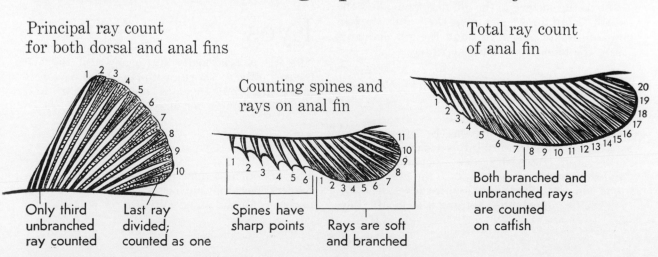

Principal ray count
for both dorsal and anal fins

Total ray count
of anal fin

Counting spines and
rays on anal fin

Only third
unbranched
ray counted

Last ray
divided;
counted as one

Spines have
sharp points

Rays are soft
and branched

Both branched and
unbranched rays
are counted
on catfish

Scales

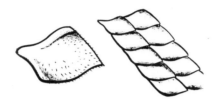

Ganoid scales

Diamond-shaped scales are found on some primitive, bony fishes. Enamel-like ganoin covers scales.

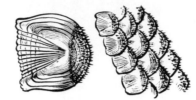

Ctenoid scales

Tiny spines on scale surface, serrated edge, give fish a rough feel. Bony plates overlap for flexible armor.

Cycloid scales

Smooth, usually circular scales covered with antiseptic mucus which prevents fungus growth.

Tails

Heterocercal fin of sturgeon

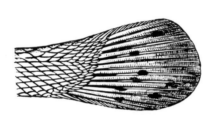

Abbreviate heterocercal fin of gar

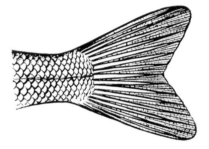

Homocercal fin of perch

Gills

Gills are a fish's primary breathing apparatus. At regular times the fish draws in a mouthful of water and forces it through the gill chambers and out the gill openings. Tiny blood vessels close to the surface in the gill filaments allow the blood to obtain oxygen from the water. Carbon dioxide waste passes through the gill filaments from the blood back into the water.

Lateral line

This visible raised tube on the side of a fish stretching from head to tail is a specialized sensory system. Beneath it lies a network of pores and sense organs, connected to the nervous system, which monitor vibrations in the water, warning the fish of enemies, helping it to locate prey.

Nostrils

The nostrils generally appear as two openings or pits on each side of the snout. They have no connection with breathing, but contain nerve cells which serve as organs of smell.

Eyes

The iris is practically stationary and the eye focuses only at short distances. Most vision is monocular, but the eyes see movements and shapes in all near-by directions at once.

Fins

The dorsal and anal fins act as anti-roll stabilizers, pectoral and pelvic fins aid in turning, and the tail can steer, stabilize, or propel.

Coloration

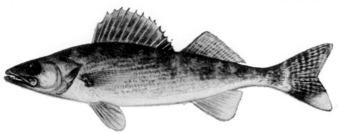

The coloration of a fish varies in different localities, sometimes even in the same lake. This walleye is a typical color in the muddy water of its southern range. Turbid water makes colors lighter.

The same species is nearly black in the brown bog water of some northern lakes. Color of water and bottom affects fish's coloration. Some fish, chameleonlike, change colors to match surroundings.

Coloration of channel catfish during life cycle

7-day-old egg

Eggs freshly laid are milky yellow, maturing to a pinkish color.

Enlarged

Enlarged

Larval stage

Translucent fry, 4 days old, carry egg's yolk (yellow) as food source.

Heavily spotted juveniles, called "fiddlers"

Young catfish show a distinctive black edge on the dorsal, adipose, caudal, and anal fins. This is lost as they mature. Green and yellow colors become grayish or brownish in larger fish.

Non-spawning adult

As channel catfish mature they tend to lose their spots. Both sexes look alike except during the spawning season. The females carry such a large mass of eggs that they become quite heavy bellied before spawning.

Male spawning color

Many spawning male channel catfish are mistakenly identified as blue catfish due to their changes in coloration. Besides color change, muscles on top of head and shoulder enlarge, and lips thicken and darken.

Chapter **6** # Fresh-water fishes of North America

Primitive fish families

Equally important to skill in handling a rod and reel, is a basic understanding of the angler's opponent—the fish. Many anglers catch fish though they may lack the knowledge to appreciate fully the marvelous mechanism they remove from their hook. Many may not know the proper name currently in use, or how to distinguish between similar species. Because of this lack of knowledge, they are often found fishing at a time and place unsuitable for the species of fish they are after.

More than 600 species of fresh-water fishes found in North America have been classified into families for identification. To help fishermen increase their interest and enjoy more pleasure from the sport, the popular fishes in each family are illustrated and discussed in this chapter.

Fish fossils, some of which are millions of years old, are found in rocks that once were the floors of ancient seas or lakes. Long after these fossil fishes were alive, most of the fishes as we know them came into being. The development of special habits and significantly different physical structures to help them live in individual environments produced the many different fish families.

But some of the primitive fish living at present have changed little or not at all through the years. Fossils of gars, for instance, are identical to those fish swimming in rivers and lakes today. The primitive fishes are not an especially handsome family, but they are especially well endowed with peculiar characteristics that enable them to survive.

← *On Arkansas' White River, two enthusiastic anglers show off their prize catch*

Sea lamprey

Petromyzon marinus

The sea lamprey is a relic of a primitive group of fishes surviving from an era long past. This eel-like fellow has no limbs, no ribs, no jaws; its skeleton is composed completely of cartilage.

You'll never catch a sea lamprey with a rod and reel, but you may find one or more attached to fish taken with tackle. To feed, the carnivorous sea lamprey attaches itself to the body of a fish with its tooth-lined "suction-cup" mouth and rasps through the scales and flesh with its file-like "tongue." This parasite draws blood from its helpless host, eventually killing the fish or weakening it to the extent that it cannot catch food and eventually dies.

Destruction of valuable sport fish

Although the sea lamprey has inhabited the Great Lakes Region above Niagara Falls for less than three decades, it has destroyed almost all of the millions of lake trout which once inhabited these waters. Other species of fish have also suffered depletion.

The effective breeding of the sea lamprey has made it impossible until now to control this parasite. During spring they work their way up tributary streams to spawn; eggs are laid and fertilized in shallow pits on gravelly riffles. A female lamprey may carry 50,000 or more eggs within her body. In a few days

the young appear and float downstream to calm water where they lodge in mud. The young sea lamprey spends several years as a larva burrowed into the mud, feeding on minute materials found in the oozy bottom. When the larva has reached about six inches in length, it changes into the adult form of the sea lamprey, which, after parasitic growth in large lakes or the sea, attains a size from 15 inches to 3 feet.

Until recently, biologists have used electric weirs to stop the adult sea lamprey from entering streams to spawn, but this procedure does not control the larvae already in the mud bottom of the stream. Now a new chemical has been discovered which, though harmless to other fish, kills the larval lampreys. Scientists are at last hopeful that this fish killer can be controlled. Only the sea lamprey, the villain in this family, is regarded as a significant pest. Some species make good bass bait.

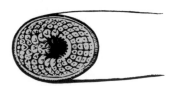

The sea lamprey has a round, sucking disc with sharp horny teeth; two separated dorsal fins, seven pairs of gill pores.

Distribution: Grand Banks, Gulf of St. Lawrence down eastern coast of the United States to Florida; in all of the Great Lakes.

Local names: Lamperns, lampers, eels (a misnomer), lamper eels, bloodsucker.

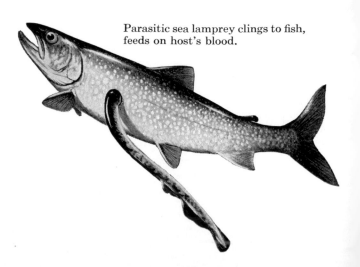

Parasitic sea lamprey clings to fish, feeds on host's blood.

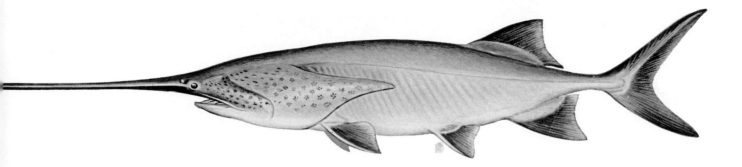

Paddlefish

Polyodon spathula

There's no mistaking a paddlefish from other fresh-water fishes. His most distinguished feature is a paddle-like snout that makes up one-third of his body length. This long snout serves no known function; if it's accidentally broken off, the fish suffers no ill effects.

In spite of his awesome appearance, the paddlefish is harmless. The diet of this primitive fish is limited to such small, soft materials as crustaceans, plankton, and insects. When feeding, the paddlefish swims with its large mouth agape, and scores of long, slender gill rakers enable it to strain a multitude of tiny organisms from the water.

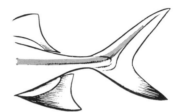

Long paddle-like snout; fish is smooth-skinned.

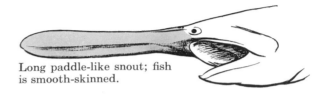

The cartilaginous vertebral column of the paddlefish extends into the long, upper tail lobe.

An unusual angling method

This feeding habit makes the paddlefish an unlikely candidate for a baited hook. The usual method of catching this fish is to use a stiff rod and heavy reel to drag an unbaited treble hook, weighted with heavy sinkers, slowly across the bottom of the stream or lake, giving strong jerks at short intervals until a fish is snagged.

The paddlefish—ranging in adult size from 3 to 6 feet long, and weighing 30 to over 100 pounds—is considered good to eat if only the light-colored meat is used. The eggs are used for caviar.

When cleaning paddlefish, first cut around the base of tail (caudal peduncle) but not all the way through. Then pull out on the tail with twisting motion to remove the elastic notochord—a long, white cord full of liquid.

Boating this fish takes a husky heave

When caught, a paddlefish is not a top fighter, but his weight makes up for what he lacks in spirit. The long snout comes in handy when it's time to boat one of these fish at Fort Randall Dam, South Dakota.

Distribution: Mississippi River system and other large gulf rivers.

Local names: Spoonbill cat, boneless cat, shovelnose cat.

White sturgeon

Acipenser transmontanus

Lake sturgeon

Acipenser fulvescens

Rows of bony plates ahead of tail are separated by naked strips. Dorsal fin has 35 to 39 rays; anal fin 30 to 38 rays.

Shovelnose sturgeon

Scaphirhynchus platorynchus

Stem of tail completely covered with bony plates. Sometimes has thin thread on upper lobe of tail.

Distribution: Pacific Coast of United States and Canada from California north to Alaska. Common in Columbia River System.

Local names: None

Four barbels under snout, closer to tip than to mouth. There are 11 or 12 bony plates on back, ahead of dorsal fin.

Upper lobe of tail longer than lower lobe as in all sturgeons. Dorsal fin has 44 to 48 rays; anal fin 28 to 31 rays.

Distribution: Hudson Bay to the Mississippi Valley, west to Missouri, Nebraska and Kansas.

Local names: Rock sturgeon, red sturgeon, rock fish.

Snout of the lake sturgeon is bluntly cone-shaped. The fish has four barbels under snout, small eyes.

Distribution: Mississippi and Alabama basins and Missouri River to Montana.

Local names: Hackleback, switchtail, sand sturgeon, flathead sturgeon.

Snout of this sturgeon is flattened and shovel shaped. Barbels are on lower side of snout.

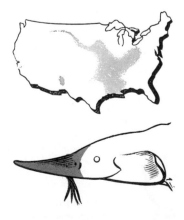

For years sturgeons have been caught by commercial fishermen for the fresh fish market as well as a source of roe for caviar. In fairly recent years they have gained the respect of sport fishermen for their fighting characteristics at the end of a line. However, declining numbers of most species of sturgeon have forced restrictive laws governing sturgeon fishing in most areas.

These laws came just in time to save the largest fresh-water fish in North America, the white sturgeon. This fish grows very slowly and as a result of heavy commercial netting years ago its numbers are relatively few today. It inhabits salt water and brackish water, though it usually prefers deep holes in large fresh-water rivers of western North America.

Any type of strong tackle can be used to catch this huge fish. Surf-fishing gear with 50 pound test line is often favored. The sturgeon isn't finicky about bait, almost anything edible will do. In some areas, smelt are used.

The lake sturgeon usually inhabits fresh water but is occasionally found in brackish water. Before our present conservation laws were in force, this sturgeon was important to commercial fishermen who sold both the meat and roe.

Most examples of this species taken on sport tackle weigh less than 50 pounds but specimens topping 200 pounds have been recorded. A variety of baits can be used, with worms and small fish the most popular choices.

Unlike the lake sturgeon, the shovelnose sturgeon is rarely hooked by sport fishermen. If he is caught, it's usually accidentally when an angler is fishing for some other species. The shovelnose prefers river bottom living where the channel has a strong current. One of the spots anglers catch these fish is below dams in major rivers while fishing for catfish or walleyes. Much smaller than either the white or lake sturgeon, it rarely exceeds 3 feet in length. The meat of the shovelnose is very good to eat.

Alligator gar

Lepisosteus spatula

Shortnose gar

Lepisosteus platostomus

Snout width between the alligator and longnose gars. At nostrils, snout wider than eye diameter.

Distribution: Large, turbid rivers of central United States, from Montana to the Gulf of Mexico.

Local names: Short bill, stub-nose gar.

Longnose gar

Lepisosteus osseus

Long narrow beak, snout width at nostrils less than eye diameter.

Distribution: Dakotas eastward to Vermont, south to Florida and Mexico. Most common in lower Mississippi drainage.

Local names: Needlenose, scissorbill.

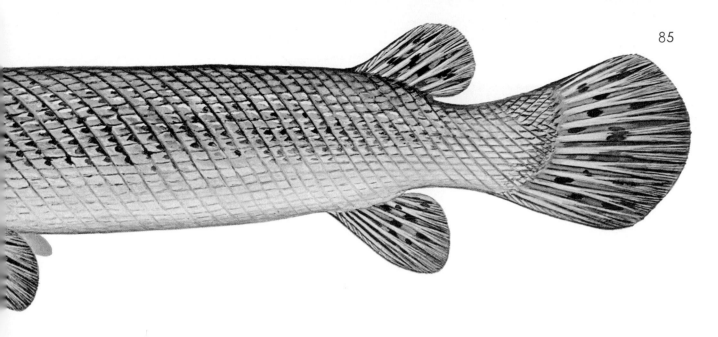

Distribution: Missouri south, in rivers flowing into Gulf of Mexico.

Local names: None

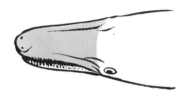

The alligator gar can be identified by its large size and broad duck-shaped snout.

All gars have the same type of diamond shaped scales. Gar scales are so hard Indians once used them for arrow tips.

The alligator gar, one of the largest North American fishes, occasionally reaches a length of over 8 feet and tops 300 pounds. It inhabits deep holes below sand bars in the channels of slow-moving streams or rivers. Fishing for it on a hot, murky day in a southern river is slow business.

This gar fights a rolling, jumping battle and can slash any line in seconds with the sharp edges of its teeth and armor-plated scales. To take this fish most anglers use stout tackle plus about 15 feet of piano wire for a leader. Carp or drum serve as cut bait.

Experienced anglers know to be patient when the alligator gar chews on their bait and then grabs it, stripping off as much as 50 yards of line. The fish usually has the bait in its bony mouth at this time and a hook will only scrape out if one strikes now. After stopping its run, the gar will swallow the bait and begin to move again. This is the time to set the hook! The battle is on, and it may last for a long time.

When the fish is tired and close to the boat, it is necessary to kill it in the water using a pistol or a blow on the head with a sharp instrument. This monster boated alive can make a wreck out of boat and angler. The jaws, studded with nail-sharp teeth can multilate an arm or leg. Since the meat is not good to eat and the

roe is poisonous, most anglers release this fish in the water by cutting the leader, being certain to keep their hands away from the jaws.

The longnose gar is a cunning bait stealer in northern waters, but with a great deal of patience, can be caught. Some fishermen still fish on hot days when the kids are hoping for *any* kind of fish to bite.

Some methods of fishing for longnose gars are quite unique. One is to use a short piece of nylon rope, unraveling the end to free the many threads. The rope is tied to the fishing line, using no hooks, and cast ahead of a surfaced gar. The gar strikes the rope and entangles its small, sharp teeth in the threads. Before it can get untangled the fisherman hauls it into the boat. Another method utilizes a wire noose with the bait in the center. When the gar attempts to get the bait, the noose is jerked tight around its nose.

The shortnose gar affords little or no angling possibilities in most areas.

Bowfin

Amia calva

The long, single dorsal fin reaches more than half the length of its body. Oval bony plate appears on its throat. The black spot on tail sometimes is absent.

The bowfin is the only living member of what once was a large family of fishes. It is the last of a family that died off long ago; its relatives are now fossils.

When you catch a bowfin you are in for a hardy battle. Many a fishing rod has been broken by this stubborn, sulking fighter. Even after it's exhausted and hauled into your boat you must watch out for its bite.

Few sportsmen fish intentionally for the bowfin yet they are liable to catch it without trying, for this cannibal will take nearly any type of plug or live bait. It is frequently caught on worms, night crawlers, minnows, chubs, frogs, or crayfish. Bowfin feed on all kinds of fish and are considered so destructive that in some areas they are regarded as pests.

The bowfin steers clear of cold water and is usually found in sluggish waters of lakes, rivers, swamps, and lagoons—often in water that would kill other sport fish. Like the gar it has a specialized lunglike air bladder for alternate breathing. It frequently comes to the surface to gulp air, and in very warm weather is likely to drown if deprived of atmospheric air.

Veteran anglers fish for it on the hottest days in stagnant, muddy water. Experienced fishermen can tell where a bowfin is feeding from the rising air bubbles and its occasional roll to the surface for air. Once these signs are spotted, an angler may throw the lure right in front of the fish, dragging it through the mud where he is feeding. Weighted bucktails and pork-rind eels are often used with spinning rods to increase the sport of catching a heavy fish on light tackle. The bowfin has a great surge of power at the beginning of the fight so treat him with respect as he takes off on a rampage.

This fish's muddy to green color is sometimes faintly iridescent. The black spot on the male's tail is usually rimmed with yellow or orange. The female's spot is without the edging and is sometimes missing.

Large bowfin occasionally reach a length of 3 feet and may weigh more than 8 pounds. The usual length, however, is around 2 feet.

This throwback to another age is edible, but the flesh is soft. Bowfin is best smoked or marinated in highly seasoned sauce before cooking. Even with these cooking methods anglers won't find this meat as tasty as that from many other kinds of fresh-water game fish.

Distribution: From Great Lakes to the Gulf. Occurs in St. Lawrence-Champlain basin in Quebec and Vermont. West of the Appalachians to Florida and Texas.

Local names: Grindel, grennel, spottail, dogfish, mudfish, lake lawyer.

Sport fishing for bowfin provides a day of excitement, a test of angling skill→

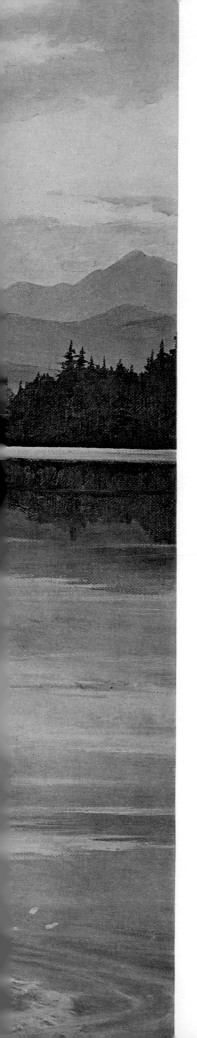

Salmon, trout, grayling, and whitefish family

At one time salmon and trout were classified in one family, and grayling and whitefish in separate families. Today, as a result of extensive research and of a clarification of identification characteristics, these four groups are classified as a single family.

The various species of trout and salmon provide many sportsmen with some of their greatest fishing thrills. These cold-water fishes, packed with energy, can make worthy tests of any fisherman's skill.

In contrast to the widely scattered trout and salmon, the arctic grayling is a fish of limited range, closely related to the whitefish and trout. Grayling inhabit wilderness areas, and attempts to stock them in water handy to civilization have met with little success. It is the only American species in its particular genus.

There are 21 species of whitefishes in North America, but only 5 are of special interest to fishermen—lake whitefish, cisco, mountain whitefish, round whitefish, and inconnu. Of this group the cisco and round whitefish are frequently fished for extensively in the Great Lakes region, because of their excellent flavor.

Chinook salmon—one of our great sporting fish

← The exact destination and the reasons for the departure of migrating salmon to the sea are intriguing unknowns pursued by ichthyologists. Returning from the sea in the final stage of their life cycle, salmon fight their way up streams toward ancestral spawning grounds. At this time fresh-water anglers get a chance for a prime specimen.

Chinook salmon

Oncorhynchus tshawytscha

In size the chinook is the granddaddy of all salmon. This game fighter may top the scales at as much as 80 pounds although the average fish caught by anglers weighs much less.

The life history of the chinook salmon is one to ponder. As the female lays about 5,000 eggs in the gravel bottom of shallow streams, the eggs are fertilized by the male. The parent fish then die; they have completed their life cycle. Though the eggs have a 20 to 40 per-cent mortality, the largest mortality occurs to the fry during fresh-water feeding stages with lack of food and predation responsible for most losses.

The young chinook feed on nymphs and larvae as they drift downstream, sometimes the full distance of lengthy rivers like the swift Yukon or Columbia to the ocean. After reaching the sea, those coming out of the Columbia generally drift northward with the Davidson current along the Continental Shelf. At first they eat plankton and small shrimp, changing their diet to herring and other small fish as they grow larger. The average size for a two-year-old is around two feet in length, reaching three feet in three or four years.

After four years the chinook have traveled up to and past the Queen Charlotte Islands. Full grown, they turn back toward their spawning grounds making the trip of over 700 miles to the

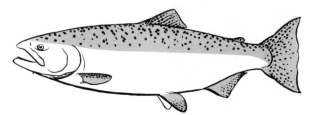

Many spots on upper body and fins. Body is deep. Spots occur on top of head. Anal fin is longer than it is high. Anal ray count generally runs to 16.

mouth of the Columbia River in three to four months. Unlike other salmon, chinook spawning runs are made in either spring, summer, or fall. Why some fish choose one season over another for spawning remains a mystery. Once at the mouth of the river they head toward the same tributary stream in which they were born. As they migrate upstream, the sheen of the chinook changes from silver to hues of brown and purple. Only a small percentage of the original run survive fishermen, rapids and waterfalls, and man-made dams to reach their destination.

Their fins mangled, their flesh now soft, bruised, and undesirable for eating, the chinook arrive at their ancestral spawning grounds, energy spent. They have just enough life in them to dig a gravel nest in which to spawn.

Distribution: Coast line and rivers of California, Oregon, Washington, Alaska, British Columbia.

Local names: Spring salmon, king salmon, tyee salmon.

Fishing for chinook in salty, brackish, or fresh water is exciting sport. Contrary to what many fishermen believe, elaborate equipment is not needed to catch this fish. But a strong rod and line are desirable.

The chinook can be caught with a variety of fishing methods. Spinning or casting with lures are favored by river and stream fishermen. The current will usually provide enough action for the lure. If the current is too slow, a slow retrieve of the spoon or plug will work; a jerk at intervals is often effective.

River mouths where these salmon enter the ocean are likely spots in which to find chinook. Deep trolling live bait—usually herring—is favored here. A dodger—metal flasher in silver, brass, or enamel finish—can be attached ahead of the natural bait to attract salmon. Care should be taken to weigh the bait properly in order that the action of the dodger isn't destroyed. Since the chinook feeds at great depths, many anglers use wire lines to provide greater strength in fighting both fish and water resistance.

Various methods can be used for still fishing. Heavily weighted bait—often a long piece of flesh cut from the side of a bait fish—cast into the water will be kept active by the current. If the current is sluggish, the bait is retrieved with a slow stop-and-go action.

A beautiful chinook is a great prize

Landing one of these giants may take half an hour or more depending upon the weight of tackle used. Fish may fight underwater, at the surface or near surface.

A helping hand is welcome when landing fighting coho salmon from a boat

Women aren't necessarily the weaker sex when Dad is attempting to get a lunker into the boat. This fish was taken on a fly rod in one of the many rivers along the Pacific Coast inhabited by salmon on their way to fresh-water spawning grounds. Coho begin migrating in the fall with runs continuing through most of the winter months. It's not unusual to get into the midst of a school of migrating coho and catch one after another of these leaping beauties. A school of coho salmon churning the surface as they feed provides exhilarating sport for fly fishermen. For either smoking or broiling the coho salmon is delicious eating.

Coho salmon

Oncorhynchus kisutch

Of all the salmon, none fights more spectacularly when hooked than the coho. It's the favorite of anglers who like to see their hooked fish in action. This near-the-surface fighter—weighing all the way from 5 to 15 pounds—puts on quite an acrobatic show with high leaps and long runs. It may be coaxed in when tired, but one look at the fisherman's boat will renew its spirit to survive.

The willingness of the coho to take flies is another reason for its popularity. When the coho are running near the surface, they provide exhilarating sport for fly fishermen. By moving in quietly and tossing a streamer fly into their midst, an angler finds immediate action as a coho leaps high into the air to challenge his skill with a fly rod.

The coho will often hit lures when flies won't attract it. Spoons, spinners, and a number of other types of artificial lures probably account for the greatest number of coho caught by hook and line fishermen.

Tackle used for coho salmon need not be as

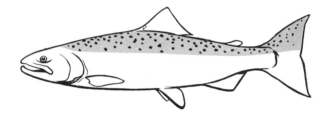

The coho salmon has dark spots on the back and upper tail. Body conformation of the coho is smaller and more slender than the chinook salmon.

heavy as that required for catching chinook. Spinning tackle and small lures are becoming increasingly popular with coho anglers. Many fishermen get best results by slowly trolling a streamer fly near the surface.

Although young coho are available in inland waters throughout most of the year, it is not until fall when mature fish return, fat from 18 months feeding at sea, that coho fishing is at its peak. Coho spawn later in the year than chinook, moving into the fresh-water streams in October and November and spawning sometimes as late as February. They also prefer smaller streams than the larger salmon. After the young cohos hatch they remain in fresh water for a year or more before heading out to sea.

The upper jaw of spawning male coho salmon hooks downward, more pronounced than in other members of this family; the lower jaw turns up to a lesser degree. Old-timers refer to the mature male coho as "hooknose" indicating a prime, highly prized specimen. In recent years this term indicates either sex in a run of coho fresh from the sea and ready to spawn.

Distribution: Coastal areas of Pacific Ocean from California to Alaska.
Local name: Silver salmon.

Pink salmon

Oncorhynchus gorbuscha

The pink salmon is not only prized commercially for its delicately flavored pink flesh, but has proved itself an excellent sport fish. It's less complex than the other members of its family, migrating only a short distance up fresh-water streams to spawn. Spawning occurs in fall with the eggs hatching the following spring; most of the young salmon immediately begin their migration to the sea.

Little is known of the pink salmon's ocean life, but it matures after two years and returns to fresh water to spawn. A trait peculiar to pinks is that their annual spawning runs vary widely in numbers over a two-year period with the majority of fish arriving on alternate years.

During spawning not only does the male's upper jaw become hooked as in other spawning salmon, but a large bony hump appears on its back from behind the head past the dorsal fin. This spawning characteristic is responsible for its local name humpback or "humpy." The female remains comparatively streamlined.

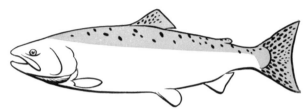

The scales of the pink salmon are much smaller than those of other salmon. Its body feels smooth, has large oval spots on tail and back.

The pink is the smallest of the salmons averaging about 18 inches in length and about 4 pounds in weight at maturity. A few specimens are caught weighing up to 10 pounds, but these are considered exceptionally large fish and a prize for any lucky angler. Spoons, spinners, and fresh bait are used frequently by sports fishermen to attract the pink salmon.

Distribution: Pacific Coast north from Oregon to Northern Alaska.

Local names: Humpback, humpy, haddo, holia.

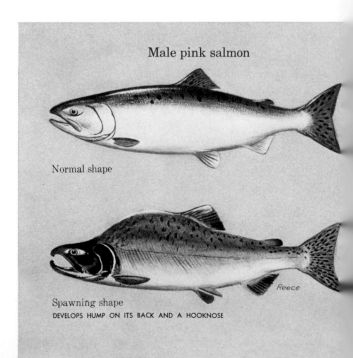

Male pink salmon

Normal shape

Spawning shape
DEVELOPS HUMP ON ITS BACK AND A HOOKNOSE

Spawning color

Chum salmon

Oncorhynchus keta

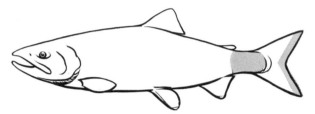

Similar in shape to the coho salmon but the tail is more deeply forked. Base of the tail is slender and rounded. Coho has wider and flatter base of tail. Anal rays number 13 or 14.

Chances are you won't have much competition when you fish for chum salmon. It has never been particularly popular with sport fishermen, perhaps because of its limited range. But its excellent fighting characteristics and willingness to hit artificial lures may eventually gain more attention. Red and white spoons and spinners are especially successful in catching this fish.

The chum averages a little larger in size than the pink salmon. A typical mature chum measures about 25 inches in length and weighs 9 to 10 pounds. But it's not unusual to find one ranging up to 20 pounds. The chum's pink or yellow flesh, lighter than most salmon, makes excellent eating. Commercial fishermen favor the chum for canning and the fresh fish market.

In the southern part of its range the chum salmon spawns in November and December, whereas farther north in Alaska large spawning runs take place in August. Chum of the southern range do not migrate far from the sea, spending only 2 to 4 months of the life cycle in fresh water. His Alaska brother, however, has been

known to travel 1,000 miles up the Yukon River.

When the chum returns to fresh water to spawn, it undergoes several changes. The shape of its body becomes less streamlined, with the head and back more angular. The jaws, especially in the male, become hook-shaped and the body color changes from silver with a bluish back to dark green with vertical reddish or purple streaks and spots. As in other Pacific salmon during spawning, chum do not feed, but live off body fat stored at sea. Fishermen and scientists are still puzzled as to why salmon hit lures at this period of their lives.

After hatching, the young salmon—called alevin—remains in the hollows among the gravel, gaining nourishment from the yolk sac attached to its belly. After the sac is expended and absorbed into the body, the parr migrates to salt water. The chum usually remain in the ocean 3 or 4 years before returning to the parent stream to spawn. Some have been known to return at a little over two years, but this is believed to be the exception, rather than normal practice of this salmon species.

Distribution: From Oregon northward along coast to North Alaska.

Local names: Dog salmon, chums, calico salmon, hayko.

Sockeye salmon

Oncorhynchus nerka

The sockeye differs from other salmon in that it is rarely caught at sea with either live bait or artificial lures. But it becomes more vulnerable during the spawning runs and may be taken by anglers in rivers and streams. The spawning male, red and physically distorted from its original beauty, has a pugnacious nature at this period and, disregarding its usual caution, readily hits lures. When hooked, it leaps, swims rapidly, and puts up one of the strongest battles of any fish its size.

Surprisingly enough, at present few anglers tackle this sport, but in Alaska where sockeyes are plentiful, more sportsmen will be fishing for this game fighter as the state develops.

While feeding in salt water the sockeye takes

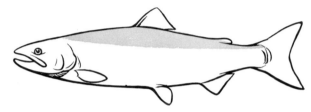

Sockeye has slender body, a few tiny specks on back but without spots as found on other salmon. Spawning males have green head and orange-red body.

on a silver color with a greenish-blue back. At spawning time important changes occur in the male: its color turns to bright red with a green head, a slight hump appears in its back, its teeth grow larger, and its snout elongates and becomes hooked. Spawning usually occurs in rivers and streams that empty into lakes.

Although the sea-going sockeye is of limited interest to hook and line fishermen, the land-locked form of the sockeye—called kokanee—is of great sporting importance. Found only in lakes and taken on light tackle, the kokanee is a game little fighter. It's similar in appearance to the salt-water sockeye, but much smaller in size, averaging around one pound at maturity, which makes it just right for pan frying. And it is a delicious fish when smoked.

Schools of kokanee attract anglers

These fish feed on plankton near the water's surface in winter and spring. Fishing is best in spring before water warms, and schools of kokanee go deep.

Spawning color

Kokanee remain in fresh water their entire 4-year life cycle, living in compact schools. They feed primarily on plankton, and do not compete with other trout for food. Spawning takes place in September through November at which time the small silver fish change to bright red and migrate into streams feeding the lake they inhabit; or at times spawn along the lake-shore. After spawning the kokanee dies.

This form of sockeye abounds in British Columbia, Idaho, Oregon, and Washington. Transplantings have been successful in some California lakes, but in a great many other areas, stocking has not been promising.

The best kokanee fishing comes in spring and early summer while they and their plankton food supply are near the surface. The plankton is most plentiful at 50°, so take along in your tackle box a fishing thermometer for measuring underwater temperatures and fish for kokanee at this level. Trolling with small spinners and spoons is the most frequently used method of catching these silver trout. Many fishermen rig a long string of spoons or spinners with a hook and worm at the end.

A bait and hook combination also produces successful still fishing. Sometimes a combination of natural baits such as a piece of worm with salmon eggs is productive when either bait used singly fails. Bait fishermen attempt to locate a school of kokanee, then anchor over the area and still fish; other boats soon join the fun.

Distribution: From the Columbia River north to Alaska.

Local names: Red salmon, blueback salmon, kokanee, blueback, silver trout, little red fish.

Sockeye salmon at spawning time

Sockeye rarely migrate up a river or stream which → doesn't have a lake or lakes along the route. Fish spawn in a stream just above or below a lake.

Atlantic salmon

Salmo salar

The scientific name of the Atlantic salmon is derived from a Latin word meaning "to leap." And leap they most certainly do, whether going upstream to spawn or trying frantically to dislodge the fishermen's lure.

The Atlantic salmon, at sea between spawning periods, is a beautiful silver fish with a dark, blue-steel back and many dark spots on its head and body. After spending some time in fresh water during spawning periods, the adults change to a reddish-olive color with large dark spots. Males become spotted with red or orange and their jaws lengthen into a beak similar to spawning Pacific salmon, with only the tips of the jaws touching.

A variety of lures attract this salmon; however, taking it on a dry fly is often considered the pinnacle of salmon fishing and is the required method of fishing in some areas. Wet flies and streamers can be effective at times as can a number of spoons and spinners.

Once the salmon hits either lure or fly, the angler is in for fast, tackle-straining action. Heavy tackle is often used since these fish are strong, leaping fighters that may weigh 10 to 20 pounds; 30 or 40 pounders are occasionally caught in North America.

Little is known about the life of the Atlantic salmon at sea, the distance they travel or their exact migration area. But periodically, these salmon enter fresh water, with spawning occurring in late fall in headwaters of streams. The female digs quite a large nest in the loose gravel or sand of the stream bed. Some eggs are laid in the nest, fertilized immediately by the male fish, and covered. The female then often excavates one or more new sites and repeats the spawning process.

The run upstream to the spawning area and the ordeal of spawning results in the death of some of these salmon. Males are especially affected because they fight constantly during spawning. But unlike the Pacific salmon, not all of this species dies after spawning. Surviving fish usually return to the salt water before freeze-up although some may remain in the stream through the winter and return to the sea early the following spring.

Eggs hatch in the spring and the resulting fry soon develop parr marks. For this reason the young salmon at this stage of life are called parr salmon and look much like trout. Parr may remain in fresh water for two or three summers before migrating to sea.

In recent years many good salmon streams have been destroyed by dams, while others have fallen into private ownership. But contrary to popular belief, many excellent portions of rivers remain open to public salmon fishing. Nonetheless, stream pollution and variable water levels which endanger the spawning runs may one day spell an end to this sporting fish. Though public agencies are struggling with the problem, the future of the Atlantic salmon is dim.

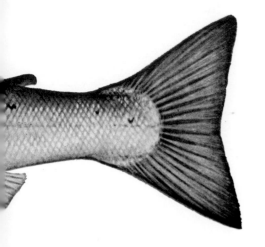

Distribution: Atlantic salmon are found from northern Quebec to Connecticut, in lakes as well as coastal regions.

Local names: Kennebec salmon, ouananiche, lake Atlantic salmon, Sebago salmon.

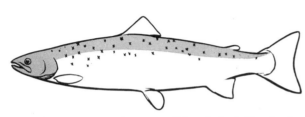

The Atlantic salmon has a small head, dark blue back, and X-shaped spots on the upper portion of his body.

The anal fin is markedly higher from base to front tip of fin than the length along the base.

On the other hand, prospects look bright for the landlocked salmon which is the same as the Atlantic salmon except that it spends its entire life in fresh water. The landlocked fish is also known as ouananiche, lake Atlantic salmon, and Sebago salmon.

This fish, originally identified in Sebago Lake, Maine, lives only in very deep, cold lakes in the northeast section of this country and Canada. Because of its popularity with anglers, the landlocked salmon has been widely transplanted. Successful stockings have been made in Quebec, Ontario, New York, Maine, and other parts of New England. In Canada it is a highly prized game fish, both in lakes and coastal rivers.

In the fall the landlocked Atlantic salmon spawns in tributary streams emptying into the lakes they inhabit. The spawning procedure is similar to that of their seagoing brothers. The fry feed on insects while in fresh-water streams, but once the young fish return to the lakes their diet consists primarily of minnows, suckers, yellow perch, and smelt.

Spring is the best time for landlocked salmon fishing as at that time they inhabit shallow water. Fishermen use flies or troll with streamers or baited hooks at this season. Later, during warm weather, this Atlantic salmon heads for deep water and can be caught by deep trolling or still fishing. The average weight for this salmon is 2 to 4 pounds, much smaller than the sea-run fish. This fish is an excellent fighter in spite of its size, and it's very good to eat.

Spawning color

Beautiful Maine scenery surrounds this angler fishing for landlocked salmon

The landlocked Atlantic salmon is a smaller fish than the sea-run variety, but what this fish lacks in size is more than made up in his fighting ability.

A hooked landlocked salmon will usually put on a spectacular aerial display in attempting to throw the hook. The Atlantic salmon will take a variety of lures. Streamers and other types of flies resembling minnows are effective because the fish feeds heavily on smelt. Many types of salmon flies used in streams are good at times for landlocks in lakes. Spinning enthusiasts can have a great time fishing for this salmon because the fish will take silver wobblers and small spoons. When the water begins to warm up in the late spring and summer, landlocked salmon head for cooler water in the deeper part of lakes.

In deep water, they can be taken by trolling silver wobblers. Because of the depth in some salmon lakes, wire lines are often used. Fish caught in deep water will not put up the spectacular fight you can expect from one caught near the surface.

Tired angler gets assistance in netting a spirited specimen of Atlantic salmon

Atlantic salmon are caught in rivers and streams which flow to the sea. Angling for this salmon is now almost entirely limited by law to fly fishing.

Taking Atlantic salmon on flies requires a somewhat different technique from fly fishing for trout. Several casts in the same spot may be needed to raise this fish. Veteran anglers place the fly beyond the rise just as in trout fishing but when the salmon takes the fly, they wait until he has turned back toward the bottom before setting the hook. A sidewise strike is best because there is less danger of pulling the hook out of the fish's mouth. A strike isn't always necessary because the fish will usually hook itself if the line is kept taut.

When hooked, the salmon should be allowed to run. The wise angler keeps tension on the line, but not enough to break the line or tear out the hook. Since there is less danger of the fish throwing the hook when under the water, fishermen often ease tension slightly to encourage the salmon toward the bottom. Keep downstream from fish so it fights against the current.

Out he comes, still fighting!

This fisherman on the Yellowstone River in Montana is enjoying the ultimate in trout fishing, taking a brown trout on a dry fly in fast water. The brown trout will also take live bait.

What a scrappy beauty!

← Any fisherman would be proud of this prize. The brown trout is not as easy to catch as some species of trout, but is worth fishing for since it is a spunky fighter and a shrewd opponent.

Brown trout

Salmo trutta

When the brown trout was introduced into North America many fishermen objected violently. They considered the brownie ugly and worthless for food; a fish that would likely kill off other trout, especially the brook trout. In fact, at the time of its introduction many sportsmen relegated the brown trout to the category some folks now save for the carp.

But times change and so do fishermen's attitudes. Civilization and pollution—not the brown trout—are now recognized as the villains responsible for the decline of the brook trout in American waters. Today the brownie is considered second to none by dry fly enthusiasts. In many parts of the United States there would be no trout fishing if it wasn't for the brownie.

The brown trout is not particularly fussy about the water it lives in. It thrives in warmer water than most other trout and can withstand more pollution. Many biologists regard it as the most satisfactory of all trout for transplanting. Brownies have been known to top 30 pounds.

This trout has large dark or brownish spots on its body, dorsal fin, adipose fin, and sometimes a few on the upper tail. Adipose fin is commonly orange.

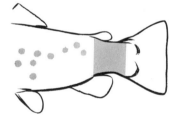

Base of tail is thick and wide. Has some orange and rusty spots. Body is yellowish or olive brown.

May flies provide the brownie's principal diet, but it will substitute other aquatic insects. It does a good share of its feeding at night—an inducement for some experienced anglers to wait until sundown before fishing.

Fishermen favor dry flies for brownies, but it goes for wet flies too; also, small spinning lures, minnows, or worms. It's not the easiest fish to catch. This spooky character requires careful presentation of fly, lure, or bait.

The brown trout can be found in lakes, streams, rivers or ponds. In some coastal areas, it runs to the sea and takes on some characteristics of the Atlantic salmon.

Distribution: Introduced in much of the United States but it's most successful in mountainous and northern sections. Southern Canada.

Local names: German brown, loch leven, brownie, Von Behr trout.

Rainbow trout

Salmo gairdneri

The rainbow is probably the best-known member of the trout family. This beauty was originally found only along the Pacific coast and in Asian waters. It's relatively easy to transplant, so today the rainbow can be caught in many parts of the world.

Rainbow trout vary widely in color markings and body shape depending upon habitat and available food. Water color may change its body coloration from silver to dark olive; fins change to brilliant red under certain food conditions. Spotting and the pink stripe along the body usually remain constant.

Fish for rainbows in both lakes and streams. In lakes, water conditions, temperature, and food supply play a large role in determining where the fish will be. In streams, look for them in pools below fast water, under logs or rocks, or at the lower end of rushing water where they lie in wait for food to be washed to them. Rainbows are more apt to be found in the swift current than brown trout.

Many Southern streams below dams of large

Pink stripe entire length of body; many dark spots on body, head, fins. No teeth on floor of gill chamber.

impoundments are sufficiently cold enough to hold transplanted trout. The release of water from the bottom of deep impoundments keeps the temperature well within the toleration range of the rainbow.

Some years ago, most rainbows were caught on fly rods. However, since the spinning rod became popular, many of these trout are caught on this type of tackle in both lakes and streams. Ordinary bait-casting rods are also used in fishing for lake rainbows.

These fighting fish will hit a variety of baits and lures. They are insect eaters so both wet and dry flies are effective. Spinners, small spoons, worms, and salmon eggs also attract this trout. For lake rainbows, spinners, usually fished deep, are popular. Like all trout, rainbows are wary fish so care must be taken not to frighten them before they have a chance to strike the lure or bait.

Rainbow trout are good fighters both on top of the water and below. At times, when hooked, these fish put on a spectacular exhibition of jumping. In addition to all of the other good qualities, rainbow trout are superb to eat.

Distribution: The rainbow trout was originally found only along the Pacific coast from Alaska to Mexico. Now, this trout is widely distributed in United States and Canada.

Local names: Steelhead, Kamloops.

Mountain trout lake

Some of the best rainbow trout fishing is found in secluded, mountain lakes. The woman angler fishing at Gnome Lake, Gallatin National Forest, finds it easier than stream fishing since she isn't bothered with snags or current, and casting is much simpler.

Early morning and late evening are usually considered to be the best times of day for trout fishing. This theory shouldn't prevent anglers from fishing at other times. Rainbows are unpredictable and may hit any time of the day.

After hooking a trout, an experienced angler keeps his rod tip high, his line tight, and tires his fish before landing it.

Keep trout cool

One of the main delights of fishing, of course, is eating the fish. The best-tasting fish is one that has been kept cool until cooked.

In the high mountains, cooling is easy if there's a handy snow bank near by. Fish kept in this fashion need not be cleaned until angler is ready to eat them. When practicable, however, it is always best to clean the fish as soon as they are caught.

New thermal-type creels help keep fish cool. If nothing else, simply cover the fish with a damp grass in a shady spot. Never leave fish lying in the sun as they spoil rapidly.

Other forms of the rainbow trout

Seagoing rainbow called *steelhead*

Large lake rainbow called *Kamloops*

The steelhead (*Salmo gairdneri*) is a rainbow trout with the wanderlust of a salmon. This fish migrates to the ocean or to large lakes such as the upper Great Lakes for a few years and then returns to fresh-water streams. Returning from the sea, it is silvery in color and is usually much larger than nonmigratory rainbow trout. After the steelhead has spent a few weeks in fresh water, it begins to darken and the pink side stripe of the rainbow becomes more obvious.

Spawning takes place in fresh-water streams in late winter or early spring. The fry spends from one to two years in its fresh-water home before migrating to the sea. Once in salt water, it may stay a few months, or as long as four years until it matures.

When the steelhead reaches maturity, some mysterious sensory mechanism, perhaps smell, is used as the fish searches for the particular stream where it was spawned. He must find the right river system, follow it until the parent stream is reached, then migrate up-stream to spawn. By marking fish with metal tags, scientists have been able to prove that these steelhead do usually return to their parent stream for spawning.

Unlike the salmon, not all steelhead die after spawning. The number of fish that survive their initial spawning run is believed to be small—perhaps under ten per cent—but research indicates that some do make several migrations to the sea and back.

An aggressive, fast water fighter

The steelhead inhabits fast white-water snow-fed streams and rivers of the Western mountain country. The beautiful rugged country is a fitting home for this aggressive fighter.

Many veteran fishermen consider the steelhead to be the toughest fighter of any fresh-water fish. Once an angler ties into one, he has his hands full. It fights above water as well as below and is amazingly strong as it fights to break free. Its long runs up- or downstream when first hooked are something no fisherman forgets. The weight of an adult steelhead usually ranges from 8 to about 25 pounds although larger specimens are occasionally caught.

Fortunately, the steelhead is found in great numbers in many streams open to the public for fishing. A strong fly rod and plenty of line on a large-size fly reel offers the greatest thrill in catching these fish. Spinning tackle or casting reels are also used.

Steelhead will hit a variety of big flies, spinners, underwater plugs, and have been caught on surface plugs. Local fishermen in the area of steelhead streams have their favorite lures and vacationing anglers will do well to get acquainted with one of these fishermen if possible. His advice can be very helpful.

Probably the best steelhead fishing occurs very early in the spring after a sudden rise in the river. Be prepared for any kind of weather ranging from snowstorms, to rain, to sunny and warm. Midwinter fishing from December through March is popular with a hardy few who don waders and heavy clothing to meet the fish on their early run upstream. Fishing from a frozen bank or an ice-crusted shallows will not only produce numb fingers and toes but often a fat, energy-packed steelhead still silver from salt water habitation.

Another form of rainbow trout

The Kamloops, originally found in British Columbia, is actually a rainbow. For years scientists classified the Kamloops as a separate species of trout until they discovered the color, number of scale rows, and other characteristics of trout could be varied simply by changing the environment and temperature of water in which the fish lived.

The Kamloops is a good example of how environment affects fish. Scale count along the lateral line is one of the measurements scientists use to identify differences between species. The scale count on the Kamloops can be reduced by raising water temperature in late embryonic development. Also when transferred from inland waters to coastal waters, it loses all the identifying features of a Kamloops and cannot be distinguished from the coastal rainbow.

The color of all trout is extremely changeable. Colors vary between different kinds of trout and even between fish of the same species. For instance, trout found in deep pools are darker than those found in shallow streams. Also, trout in fast waters may have much slimmer bodies than those found in lakes or deep pools. Some scientists believe that feeding habits also have an effect on trout color and body conformation.

The Kamloops, like the steelhead, can be taken on a variety of spinners, spoons, bucktails, big flies, and live bait. A 2-pound Kamloops is considered average, with lunker size running 4 to 8 pounds and an occasional speciman running up to 30 pounds.

Whether the fish you are after is a steelhead fresh from the sea, or a Kamloops inland, either of these forms of rainbow trout will provide the thrill of hooking a magnificent fighting fish.

A record rainbow worth bragging over

The Kamloops, like other rainbow trout, will hit a fly and other lures with a smash and a splash. This fish is a leaping fighter when hooked; his runs are long and fast. This rainbow was found in British Columbia but has been introduced into some areas of northwestern United States. Lake Pend Oreille, Idaho, where this fish was landed, has produced some very large rainbows in the past few years.

Cold weather fishing for steelheads

This fisherman has almost, but not quite, landed a beautiful steelhead. The winter and early spring spawning migrations of steelhead provide excellent fishing in a large number of western coastal streams. Spinning tackle is gaining popularity with steelhead fishermen, but many use heavy fly rods or casting rods. A cluster of salmon eggs tied to the hook with a thin wire or red yarn is the bait most commonly used.

Bright sunshine, a meandering trout stream,
magnificent mountains, blissful solitude:
There's more to fishing than catching fish.

Cutthroat trout

Salmo clarki

Anything you hear a veteran fisherman say about the cutthroat trout is probably true. As variable as the weather, it's found in coastal waters and in far inland lakes and streams, but mostly in the mountains. Few other fish have as many names as the cutthroat trout; more than 70 are recorded for him.

The cutthroat is named well; slashes of red or orange on the lower jaw identify all varieties. The exception is rare.

When compared with other species of trout, cutthroats are not large. Inland trout average 10 to 15 inches, sea-run cutthroats 16 inches, al-

Cutthroat has a long, red and orange slash on each side of throat below mouth, small teeth on floor of the gill chamber.

though some lunkers exceed 20 pounds in weight. What these trout lack in size, they make up in fighting qualities. Many anglers consider the cutthroat the ideal trout for fly fishermen.

These scrappers will hit a variety of flies, small spoons, spinners, and lures. They're not as fussy as rainbows as to type of fly used or how it's presented to them. Their principal natural foods are adult and larvae of May flies, stone-flies, caddis flies, small fish, and, in some lakes, fresh-water shrimp. One of the best natural baits a fisherman can use is a couple of worms dangling on the hooks of a Colorado spinner, jigged along to give action.

Cutthroats migrating to the sea stay close to the river mouth, traveling back and forth from fresh to salt water. In this habitat these handsome trout feed on sand fleas, snails, small crabs, minnows, and other small fish.

Distribution: All of the Rocky Mountain area, west to the Pacific Coast, from California to southern Alaska.

Local names: Alaska cutthroat, Montana black-spot, blueback trout, mountain trout, native trout, black-spotted trout, Yellowstone trout.

Various color phases of the cutthroat from major Western watersheds

The cutthroat trout has the most diversified array of color patterns of any species of trout. Formerly various stocks, each differing slightly from those of other areas, were divided into a host of subspecies. Each originally lived in its own geographic area and possessed a distinctive coloration. Now many of these have been mixed through indiscriminate stocking or have hybridized with rainbow trout, and the true native forms of cutthroat no longer are found. Environments of the watersheds may cause variations in coloration. Spawning causes additional color change which further complicates identification for the angler in the field.

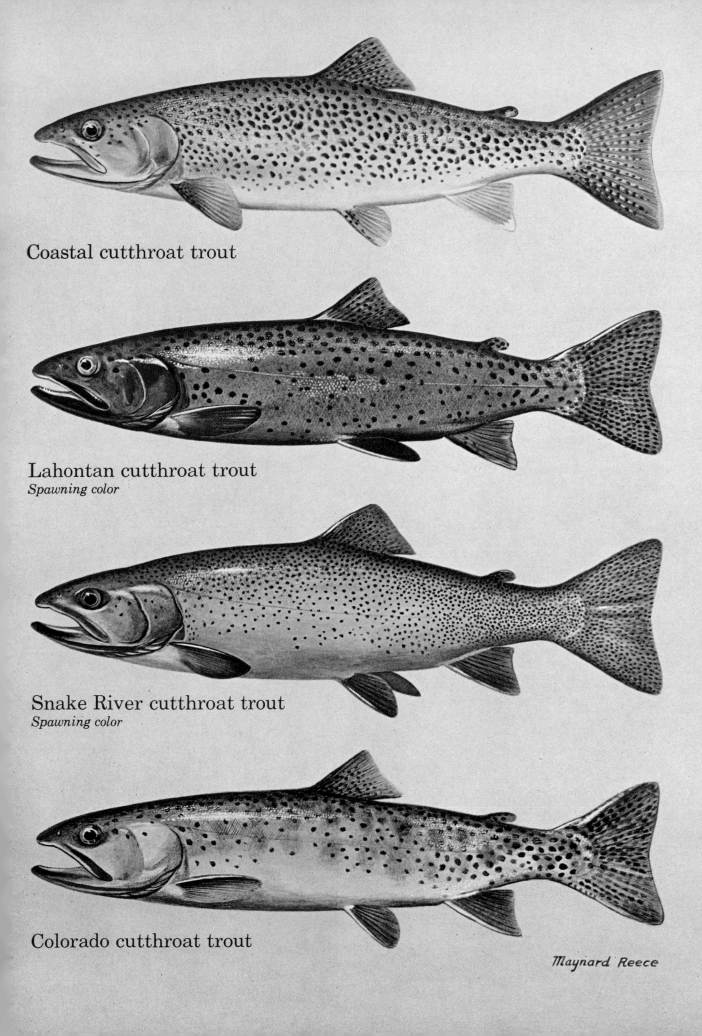

Coastal cutthroat trout

Lahontan cutthroat trout
Spawning color

Snake River cutthroat trout
Spawning color

Colorado cutthroat trout

Maynard Reece

Lunch where air is thin, goldens fat

There is no better place to eat lunch, take a drink, or fish than in a small alpine lake. These families left their base camp at a lower elevation for a day's trip to one of Wyoming's above-timberline golden trout lakes. Because of the rugged, but beautiful areas in which the golden trout is distributed, most anglers use horses to reach the high-country lakes and streams. Some dedicated trout fishermen hike into the area carrying camping equipment in packsacks.

Small angler, medium-size goldens

The development of spinning tackle has made it possi-→ ble for the non-fly rod fisherman, like this young lady, to really enjoy trout fishing. The golden trout pictured here were caught on a small, silver wobbler. Fly rod enthusiasts should try both wet and dry flies on this fish. Golden trout will sometimes prefer one over the other, depending upon their diet and location at the time the angler is fishing. Golden trout, like most other trout, can also be caught with live bait.

Golden trout

Salmo aguabonita

Although the golden trout is widely known, only a small percentage of fishermen have had the opportunity to catch this fish.

One reason for the lack of fishing pressure is the golden's limited and difficult-to-reach range. This is truly a fresh-water game fish of the mountain tops, found in high altitude lakes and streams above the timberline of the country's most rugged mountains.

Originally the golden was caught in a few small streams flowing into the Kern River in California. Since its discovery, it has been introduced into a number of western states. A peculiar thing happens to the coloration of this trout as it is transplanted to various mountain areas. Certain characteristics such as the red side stripe and white tips on lower fins remain constant. But the white tip on the dorsal fin, the yellow color on the sides, and parr marks, plus the spotting may vary greatly from lake to lake.

Golden trout are not large fish; they average 8 to 15 inches and occasionally reach 20 inches in length. The record golden caught in Cook's Lake, Wyoming, weighs 11 pounds; measures 28 inches long. What they lack in size they more than make up in beauty. Their coloration is only matched by the spectacular scenery of the surrounding terrain. Usually waters inhabited by goldens are crystal clear and on a calm day the

Black spots appear on the golden's upper body, dorsal and adipose fins, tail, and base of tail. Red stripe on side from head to anal fin has black parr marks showing. White tip on pelvic and anal fins. Sides are yellow below the lateral line.

fish can be seen cruising in search of food. They feed on insects, crustaceans, and small fish.

Difficult as it may be to reach golden trout waters, most veteran anglers agree that this fish is worth the effort. He is a good fighter at the end of a line, though he probably doesn't measure up to the rainbow's fighting spirit. Golden trout can be taken on fly rods, spinning rods, or casting tackle.

A half dozen goldens, deep fried in a skillet, turn a wilderness lakeside lunch into a feast. But be sure to take along a sandwich for lunch as these fish can be erratic in their feeding habits and it is always possible to fish all day and turn up with an empty creel.

Fishing for golden trout is usually limited to the summer months when the receding snow makes it possible to reach high altitude lakes and streams. Even then the trip to golden trout water can be rugged so anglers should take along warm clothing. A sudden snow or sleet storm is not unusual at high altitudes, and the nights are cold the year around.

Distribution: High country of California, Idaho, Oregon, Washington, Montana, Wyoming.

Local names: None.

Dolly Varden

Salvelinus malma

The Dolly Varden, important to anglers because of its size and availability, can be caught by casting or trolling. Silver spoons are especially attractive to it, as are many types of spinning lures. It readily takes wet flies and will occasionally hit dry flies.

Its principal diet includes insects, crustaceans, other fish, plus salmon and trout eggs. This latter delicacy has made the Dolly Varden unpopular in areas where salmon spawn since it is a voracious feeder. At one time commercial fishermen regarded the Dolly Varden as a threat to the salmon crop and in certain areas it was

These fishermen go after the Dolly Varden in fast moving water of the Flathead River near Kalispell, Montana.

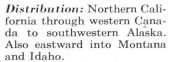

Distribution: Northern California through western Canada to southwestern Alaska. Also eastward into Montana and Idaho.

Local names: Bull trout, salmon trout, Dolly, char, red-spotted trout, western char, Oregon char.

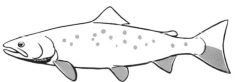

Sides of Dolly have yellow or orange spots. Front edge of lower fins is margined with white, all fins are spotless.

declared a nuisance, a bounty was paid for it.

Dolly Varden inhabit lakes, rivers, or streams. In the western coastal areas it may migrate to the sea and return to fresh water to spawn. In parts of Alaska the population of Dolly Varden is dense enough for fishermen to report two and three fish attempting to hit their lures. But in more accessible areas the population has diminished as a result of fishing pressure and the fish's willingness to hit a lure. In size it often attains 10 pounds. The world record holder weighed 32 pounds.

This fish has never been as favored among sportsmen as many of the trout. When hooked, it becomes a beneath-the-surface fighter, especially in deep water; in streams the Dolly Varden may occasionally jump, but it won't put on the spectacular aerial show of a rainbow trout. Nonetheless, it is a strong fighter who deserves more attention from fishermen.

They are using spinning tackle, but this fish can also be taken with a casting rod or fly fishing equipment.

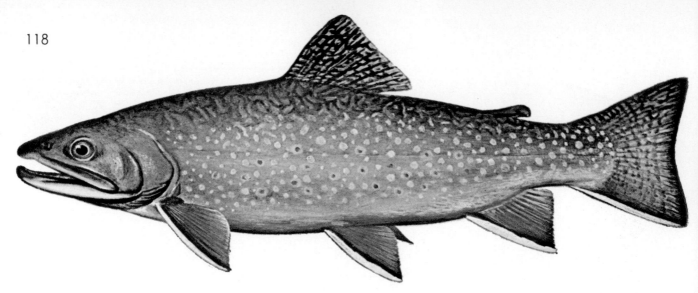

Brook trout

Salvelinus fontinalis

Since the brook trout doesn't take readily to civilization it has disappeared from much of its former natural range in New England and eastern Canada. Attempts to transplant it from its native eastern habitat to the West have been spotty in their success; plantings in mountainous areas of some southern states have been moderately better.

Brookies, or speckled trout as these fish are commonly called, thrive in cold, pure water. Such waters have grown increasingly scarce over the years. Although streams are its usual habitat, brook trout also live in cold lakes where they generally run larger in size than their stream-oriented brothers. In coastal rivers of the northeast, some brookies migrate to and from the sea.

Coloration of the brook trout varies with water conditions. Also, types of food eaten may cause color differences in the flesh. The vermiculate markings, bright spots, and colorful lower

Light, worm-like lines on dark olive back. Front part of lower fins is black with white edges. Side shows red spots circled with blue, yellow, or gray. Reddish lower fins and red belly on breeding male.

body and fins make this trout one of the most beautiful fresh-water fishes.

Brookies feed on a variety of water organisms, but their main food consists of insects. This makes them prime targets for a properly presented fly, either dry or wet. After the water cools in the fall brookies move upstream and spawn in shallow water having a gravel bottom.

This colorful trout is primarily a bottom feeder. You'll find that a wide choice of flies presented in fast, slow, or still water, will interest it. Although it doesn't grow as large as some United States trout, it's a good fighter for its weight. In Canadian waters brookies reach up to 7 pounds. In Maine and eastern Canada some fresh-water fishing enthusiasts consider large brook trout, or squaretails as they are called, as much a prize as a salmon.

Some folks clean and *skin* brookies immediately after catching and cook them to a golden brown over a lakeside fire. A half dozen small trout rolled in flour and deep fried in butter are hard to top for a wilderness meal.

Distribution: Original habitat from Ontario east to Labrador, south in the Appalachians and Georgia. Has been transplanted into most states except in the far south.

Local names: Brookies, squaretails, speckled trout.

The beauty of a New Hampshire stream makes fall fishing a delight for this family →

Lake trout

Salvelinus namaycush

The lake trout, one of many fishes native only to North American water, is the largest member of the trout group. Specimens weighing 20 to 50 pounds are caught by hook-and-line fishermen but the average fish is much smaller.

This fish inhabits only those lakes which are deep, cold, and where the water contains a large amount of oxygen. The lake trout can be taken near the surface of lakes in the spring, but once the water begins to warm, it heads for the deeper, colder parts of the lake.

While in shallow water, this trout provides great sport for fly-rod fishermen, also for bait-casting or trolling anglers. It will hit spinner-fly combinations as well as a number of other artificial lures. Spoons and wobblers are favored by many fishermen; small spinning lures are some-times effective. This trout is an excellent fighter in shallow water but rarely breaks the surface when hooked. After the battle, the angler is likely to find his line wrapped around the fish's body.

When the lake trout retreats to deep water in warm weather, a different angling technique is required. The lure must be fished very deep, just above the bottom, and it must be trolled slowly. Lake trout in warm weather may be at depths of 200 feet or more. Tackle for deep-water lake trout fishing usually consists of a stiff rod and a special reel to handle a metal line. The line can be metal or one with a metal core encased in nylon. When metal or metal core lines are used, a sinker is normally unnecessary to get the bait down to the fish. Silk or nylon lines can be used but require a heavy sinker.

Lake trout, spawning color

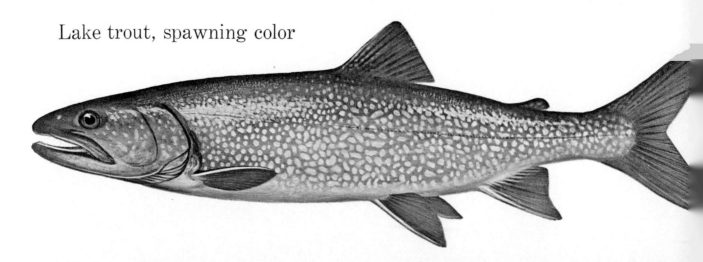

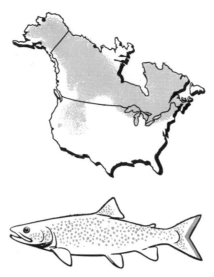

Distribution: Labrador to Alaska, southward to Montana. Throughout the Great Lakes to northern New England. Introduced in Connecticut, California and a few Western lakes.

Local names: Mackinaw, togue, laker, Great Lakes trout, gray trout, salmon trout.

Lake trout has forked tail, light gray spots on the head, body, upper fins and tail.

Lake trout caught in deep water during the summer usually do not put up as much of a battle as those taken in the spring or fall in shallow water. The fish in deep water is forced to fight the heavy line in addition to the lure. Also, the change in water pressure as the fish is brought to the surface reduces his fighting ability. For deep-water lake trout fishing, large copper or silver spoons are first choice with many experienced fishermen.

The splake is a cross between a lake trout and a brook trout and it is sometimes called a wendigo trout, or moulac. This hybrid is created by fertilizing lake trout eggs with the milt from a male brook trout at the hatchery. The survival of eggs and young is about the same as with either species. When the opposite cross is made, however, many of the fry are deformed, all die soon after hatching. Unlike most true hybrids, the splake is fertile and it is hoped that this fish will reproduce and increase in number under natural conditions.

The splake often reaches lake trout size and retains many of the fighting characteristics of both parents. It is a good sport fish with distribution in both the United States and Canada, but as yet numbers are limited. The splake, like the lake trout, makes a tasty steak.

Splake

Cross between brook trout and lake trout

Successful lake trout fisherman

This happy angler welcomes help with the net in landing his beautiful lake trout. In spring and fall lake trout swim near the surface; this prize was caught by casting from shore with a wobbling spoon.

Typical lake trout fighting action

Big lake trout often roll or spin after they are fought → to the surface. This action results in the fish entangling himself completely in the line, making it a difficult job to bring the trout to the net.

Arctic char

Salvelinus alpinus

If you are fortunate enough to fish for arctic char, you'll have an experience shared with relatively few anglers. Arctic char waters lie far to the north from Newfoundland across Hudson Bay west to Alaska. Due to its remote range, little was known about this fish until fairly recently when civilization began to push into the northern frontier.

In parts of its range the char is landlocked. This isolation has produced various forms of arctic char: Sunapee trout, blueback, and Quebec red trout. Some ichthyologists feel that every form of the arctic char is a different species, while others claim the various forms are the same species with their differences resulting from environmental change due to habitat. The American Fisheries Society, agreeing with the latter group, has lumped all forms together as one species, the arctic char.

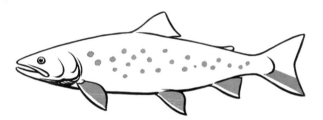

Sides have pink, yellow, or white spots; no spots on back or fins. Lower fins have white leading edges.

Breeding season for arctic char is fall. The fish migrate from sea to fresh-water streams and lakes in late July and August. Spawning occurs in September through October as the lakes begin to freeze over. In spring, after the shore ice disappears, adult char migrate back to the sea. Sometimes they will gather in the shallows along the shores of the Far North lakes, waiting for the winter's ice to break.

Spawning color

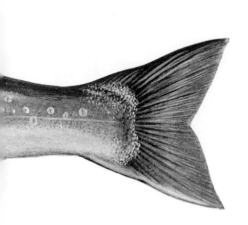

Distribution: Areas in and near Alaska and the Canadian arctic; isolated areas in New England and Eastern Canada.

Local names: Sunapee trout, seatrout, Arctic trout, blueback trout, and Quebec red trout.

The color of the arctic char varies with the type of water the fish inhabits. Fish directly from the sea are mostly silver, while in fresh water they may be bluish-gray to deep blue. The lower fins and sides in spawning fish run orange to red and the leading edges of the lower fins are white.

When hooked, the arctic char is a husky fighter that challenges a sportsman's best angling skills. It can be caught with spoons, spinners, spinner-fly combinations, or hooks baited with worms or pieces of meat. Large spoons that can be cast or trolled are favored by many char fishermen. Locating char is often as simple as looking over the side of the boat and finding it cruising many feet below the surface in the clear water it inhabits. At other times this fish will swim near the surface with fins and tail showing.

The arctic char reaches a weight of 20 pounds or more. Since these fish inhabit relatively inaccessible waters, much larger specimens may exist. Some veteran fishermen feel this figure is topped annually by Eskimos in wilderness.

Sunapee Lake, New Hampshire, is one of the few remaining spots in the United States where a landlocked variety of the arctic char can be found. Residents of the area discovered the Sunapee trout in 1880 and have protected this variety ever since. To perpetuate the remnant, New Hampshire in recent years has gone to hatchery methods, catching female fish in the fall during spawning, stripping the eggs, and artificially fertilizing them. After controlled hatching they raise the offspring to 10 inches before releasing them into the lake. Resulting specimens run to 10 pounds.

Quebec, Canada, has had similar success with their red trout. But only the future holds the answer as to whether the arctic char can continue to thrive in a landlocked environment encroached upon by civilization.

Slim speedster of the far north waters

This char was taken on a spoon at Frobisher Bay, Baffin Island, Northwest Territories. Fishing in arctic waters is limited to 2 or 3 summer months except for Eskimos netting and spearing through the ice for food.

Arctic grayling

Thymallus arcticus

Mention arctic grayling to a group of experienced fishermen and their talk soon turns to enthusiastic praise of this fish. A great part of the interest originates in the fact that the arctic grayling is of limited distribution in North America.

Relatively few anglers have had the opportunity to hook this character with the high-dorsal fin for the arctic grayling is a fish of far and lonely places. Its range is severely limited to areas where the water is cold and clear. Grayling inhabit rivers and lakes throughout Alaska, and waters east across Northern Canada to Hudson Bay. Some isolated lakes and streams in Montana also contain grayling.

Successful transplantings of arctic grayling have been made in streams and lakes in Yellowstone Park, but in other parts of the United States transplantings have met with little success. This sleek little fish was formerly abundant in Michigan but disappeared from that region in the 1930s. Subsequent stockings of grayling

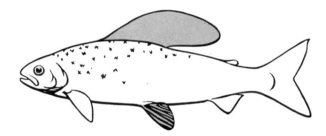

Arctic grayling can be identified by the large sail-like dorsal fin. Pelvic fins are striped. X-shaped spots appear on fore part of body.

in Michigan have been of only limited success.

This cold water beauty resembles the whitefish in shape, having the same large scales, forked tail, and small mouth. But the large dorsal fin, which looks like the fin of a sailfish, sets the grayling apart from any other freshwater game fish.

Grayling rarely exceed 10 to 18 inches in length. One of the largest fish caught on hook and line was recorded at just 4 pounds.

Spawning occurs during spring as the ice goes out in small tributary and feeder streams. Unlike the indifference of many other fish, the male grayling jealously guards the area where spawning takes place, rushing all intruders with dorsal fin erect.

Grayling are not difficult to catch. They are one of the few far-north fish that will take both wet and dry flies with consistency. Many a grayling is missed because too much slack line is allowed to develop and it hits and darts away before the fisherman can set the hook. Having a

Distribution: Alaska, Yukon, Northwest Territories, Alberta, Manitoba, Saskatchewan, British Columbia, Montana, and Yellowstone Park.

Local names: American grayling, Montana grayling.

small mouth, it is apt to nip gingerly rather than strike out viciously as some trout. Veteran anglers start setting the hook on seeing the flash instead of waiting for the strike, as man's reflex action needs a little forewarning to hit the timing of a fast strike. Spinning or casting tackle with a variety of small lures can also be used successfully for grayling.

These fish feed on grasshoppers, flies, bees, ants, stone flies, May flies, dragon flies, caddis flies, black flies, midges, beetles, and other insects. Arctic grayling have also been known to eat fresh-water shrimp, worms, and, at spawning time, even their own eggs.

When hooked, the grayling is not a strong or dramatic fighter like the salmon or rainbow. Most of his battling takes place under the surface of the water. Nevertheless, the grayling is no pushover; any fisherman who has landed one can be proud of his trophy.

Most anglers consider arctic grayling delicious to eat, and many fish for them with this sole purpose in mind. Some epicures state that grayling have a flavor suggestive of thyme.

No mistaking that dorsal fin, it's a grayling, caught near Great Bear Lake

Inconnu

Stenodus leucichthys

The inconnu, inhabiting both fresh and brackish water in the Arctic area, is isolated from all but a relatively small number of sportsmen due to its range. This predacious whitefish is known to migrate over 1,000 miles in some cases. Migration to the sea is common with the inconnu but in some large lakes such as Great Slave, the fish is landlocked.

The inconnu can be caught with spinning or casting tackle. Small, silver spinning lures are effective and spoons of fairly good size or bass plugs are hit eagerly by this fish. The inconnu is a superb sporting fish when taken on a fly rod with marabou or bucktail streamers. Though it will generally take lures readily near the surface, the angler may need to fish close to the bottom during rainstorms and hot days.

Most fishermen report inconnu meat very good to eat, others state that the flavor leaves much to be desired. Eskimos often eat it raw.

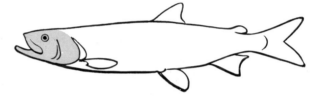

The inconnu has a long head and lower jaw protruding beyond snout similar to that of a tarpon. This whitefish has a slender silver body.

Part of the thrill of fishing for inconnu is visiting the remote Arctic lakes which this fish inhabits.

Distribution: Arctic area waters of northwestern Canada and Alaska.

Local names: Conee, cony, sheefish, cheefish.

Lake whitefish

Coregonus clupeaformis

Until about the turn of the century when sportsmen discovered that it could be caught on hook and line, the lake whitefish was taken only by commercial fishermen using nets. Today, in many areas, sport fishing for whitefish attracts many enthusiasts.

The lake whitefish averages 2 to 4 pounds and is highly prized by commercial fishermen for its excellent flavor. Huge catches of lake whitefish were once common in the Great Lakes but the sea lamprey has reduced the number of the fish in these waters.

This fish primarily inhabits deep, cold-water lakes of the north country, but is also found in several Alaskan rivers. It is caught in deep water, sometimes 70 feet or greater. In the spring the lake whitefish comes into the shallows or shoal areas to spawn, but soon returns to the deeper water where it prefers to stay.

Ice fishing for lake whitefish has gained tremendous popularity in some parts of the coun-

The lake whitefish has a blunt, overhanging snout; the small mouth is built to feed on the bottom. The fish is silvery.

Two flaps of skin are located between nostrils.

try. Live minnows are favored by ice fishermen as whitefish bait. If live minnows are not available, salted minnows make an acceptable substitute. Other baits occasionally used include cooked grain such as rice, also chopped flesh of the burbot or other fishes. Pieces of bait are often dropped through holes in the ice a few days ahead of the time a fisherman intends to try his skill; this "chumming" procedure attracts whitefish to the area.

Shoal areas and river mouths where water depth may be from 10 to 60 feet are good fishing spots in spring and fall. In summer, whitefish move into deeper water. The same bait can be used for open-water fishing in these seasons as is used during winter.

Regardless of whether whitefish are caught through the ice or during the warmer periods of the year, landing one of these fish is not always easy. The lake whitefish is not in the fighting class with the bass or trout, but the fish's soft mouth makes it difficult to handle.

Distribution:
Northern New England, through Great Lakes System, Newfoundland west to Alaska.

Local names: Great Lakes whitefish, common whitefish, whitefish, inland whitefish, shad.

Cisco

Coregonus artedii

Distribution: Great Lakes region, eastern and central Canada.

Local names: Shallow-water cisco, blueback, grayback, freshwater herring.

For years sportsmen thought the cisco would take only baited hooks or metal lures. Recently however, fishermen discovered that the cisco will occasionally take a dry fly fished on or slightly below the surface of the water.

This speedy, small fish has a very soft mouth, so the angler must be careful to set the hook gently. Mature ciscoes average a pound although specimens up to 8 pounds have been caught.

Cisco has a sharp snout, lower jaw longer than upper.

Two flaps between the nostrils. Ciscoes are silvery in color.

Round whitefish

Prosopium cylindraceum

Fish has small mouth, tip of snout is level with eye. Lower jaw shorter than upper. Faint black blotches (parr marks) along lateral line in juveniles.

Single flap between nostrils. Dark bronze back.

Quite often in early spring trout fishermen will switch from rainbows to fishing for the round whitefish in the fast water of small streams emptying into large lakes. The meat is delicious and a lot of sport is derived while snow is still spotting the landscape.

Live or salted minnows usually provide the best fishing, although some anglers use cooked grain for bait. The round whitefish will also hit flies at certain times of the year. Set the hook gently, since this is another soft-mouthed fish.

Distribution: Great Lakes region, northern New England, eastern and northern parts of Canada to Alaska.

Local names: Menominee, pilot fish.

Mountain whitefish

Prosopium williamsoni

The sporty little mountain whitefish comes into its own in fall and winter after the trout season closes. Like other members of its family, it has a very soft mouth and must be played carefully. For ice fishing, anglers favor hellgrammites and maggots, but in open water this whitefish will take wet or dry flies.

The mountain whitefish is present in both lakes and streams. Occasionally streams overpopulated with mountain whitefish suffer from lack of food for trout. Therefore, in some areas they are considered pests.

Spawning occurs in fall and early winter with the fish in lakes moving into streams to spawn over gravel and riffle areas. The fry hatch in early spring. Mature mountain whitefish average 12 inches and weigh up to 3 pounds. Their meat compares favorably with trout.

Mountain whitefish have a small mouth with the lower jaw shorter than the upper. Fish has brown-olive back. Large adipose fin.

Single flap of skin is located between nostrils.

Distribution: Rocky Mountain area west to the Pacific coastal states and British Columbia.

Local names: Mountain herring, pea nose, Rocky Mountain whitefish.

A fine catch of whitefish and trout

Alongside this large brown trout hang two mountain whitefish. Whitefish this size are full of fight and a credit to any fly-rod angler. Both species can be caught in the same water on the same type of bait.

Mooneye, herring and smelt families

The mooneye and goldeye comprise the mooneye family. Although their value to anglers varies with the availability of more popular sport fish, these fish, nonetheless, constitute an important food source for many game fish.

The herring family, on the other hand, has 26 American species, most of which spend a good portion of their life cycles in the ocean. Many of the members of this family are comparatively small. But the American shad, which is growing in popularity among fishermen on both coasts for his willingness to take artificial lures, occasionally weighs up to 12 pounds.

Smelt fishing is a gregarious sport often shared by entire families. When schools of smelt are running, large crowds gather to harvest these small creatures which are such a delight to the appetite. In many areas smelt fries are commonplace. Whether these fish are dipped out of the streams during spawning migration or caught one at a time through the ice in winter, smelt fishing affords a top family activity that can be enjoyed by all ages.

Dipping for smelt is fun and productive

← Smelt runs provide fast, exciting sport. When the smelt run is on, entire families, almost entire populations of some towns, turn out with dip nets and buckets or tubs to get in on the harvest. Most smelt runs take place at night when thousands of these fish cram their way up small streams and rivers to deposit their eggs.

American smelt

Osmerus mordax

This small, delicious fish can be caught with dip nets or on hook and line. Great quantities of smelt are taken as the fish move into small streams to spawn. They may also spawn on shallow beaches of lakes.

Smelt can be caught by hook and line anglers fishing through the ice using very small minnows. Small flies are good warm-weather bait when schools are near the surface.

American smelt has a large mouth with canine teeth on the jaws, tongue, roof of mouth.

Tail is deeply forked and fish has adipose fin. Scales are large, thin, and easily removed.

Mooneye

Hiodon tergisus

The mooneye and goldeye, the two species in the mooneye family, are popular with only a few fishermen. Many of these fish, however, are caught by anglers fishing for other fish. Both species will take artificial flies and will hit small spinning lures. These fish feed primarily on insects, but also eat crayfish and small fish. In spring, they migrate up rivers to spawn.

Adult mooneyes measure 12 to 14 inches in length and weigh from 1 to 2 pounds. Both of these fish are edible but are not top quality.

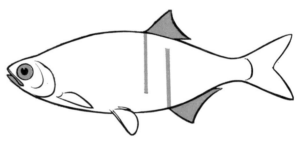

Deep-bodied and slab-sided with large eyes. Dorsal fin's front edge ahead of anal fin's front edge. Goldeye's dorsal fin starts *behind* front edge of anal fin.

Distribution: Hudson Bay and St. Lawrence-Champlain drainages, Great Lakes, Mississippi River to Alabama and Arkansas.

Local names: Toothed herring, river whitefish.

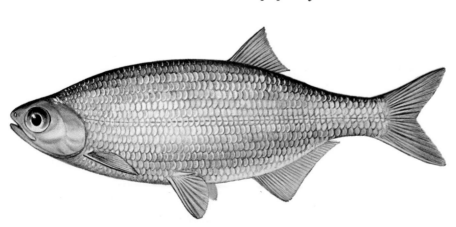

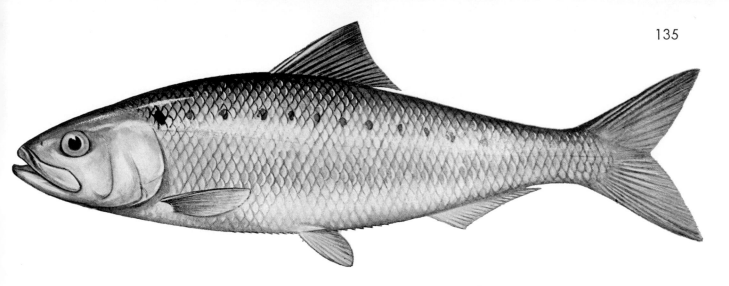

American shad

Alosa sapidissima

The shad is found on both coasts and spends most of its time in salt water. Spawning takes place from a few miles to 200 or even 400 miles up fresh-water streams and this is where most sportsmen seek it out. In the northern part of its range the shad returns to the sea after spawning, but in the southern part both male and female die.

While shad feed primarily on plankton they also eat crustaceans, tiny shrimp, fish eggs, and small fish. Small silver spoons often trolled slowly near the bottom bring results. Lead jigs are favored by many fishermen. Light colored flies are at times effective.

An adult shad reaches a length of up to 30 inches and may weigh 8 pounds. Both the fish and its roe are considered excellent food.

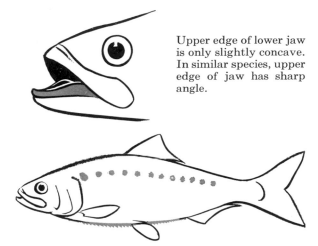

Upper edge of lower jaw is only slightly concave. In similar species, upper edge of jaw has sharp angle.

Dark spot behind the head, with indistinct spots leading toward tail. Saw-toothed edge on belly.

Shad fishing on light spinning tackle gives river angling another sport fish.

Distribution: Atlantic Coast from St. Lawrence River to St. Johns River in Florida. Introduced on Pacific Coast. Now from California to Alaska.

Local names: Shad, white shad, jack, Atlantic shad.

Pike family

For sheer stubbornness at the end of a line, it's difficult to match some of the five kinds which make up the pike family. The chain pickerel, grass pickerel, redfin pickerel, northern pike, and muskellunge are fine sporting fish, though two of them are quite small.

These five fishes have similar characteristics. They all have the same spawning habits, the same habitat preferences, and nearly the same physical shape. However, they differ considerably in color, marking, and size at maturity. The redfin pickerel, for instance, seldom exceeds a pound while the muskie may reach 50 pounds.

Members of the pike family will hit artificial lures or live bait with plenty of power—no gentle nibbling for these streamlined fighters. Often they follow the bait before striking. Once hooked, they frequently leap clear of the water attempting to throw the lure. Or they may dive to the bottom and sulk in a weed bed. Part of the fun of hooking these fish is that an angler rarely knows how they will react.

A word of caution: Once a fisherman lands a member of the pike family, he should treat the fish with respect when removing the hook. Their teeth are sharp and numerous. If fishing from a boat, tackle boxes should be kept closed. These fish usually keep fighting even after they are landed and a pike flopping around can scatter equipment far and wide.

Out it comes, a northern full of fight!

← The northern pike is usually a rugged, slashing fighter when hooked. An angler shouldn't be surprised if his lure is thrown back at him as the fish leaps to shake loose the hook from its tough mouth. Or the fish may wrap the line around a snag or in a tangle of weeds, giving him a chance to break away.

Northern pike

Esox lucius

Opercle of northern pike is without scales on lower half. Cheek is fully scaled.

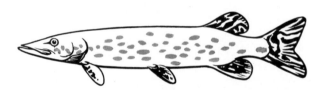

Northern pike can be distinguished by the pale spots on head and body. Dark markings appear on tail, usually on fins. Occasionally found without markings.

With the exception of the muskellunge, probably no other fresh-water game fish is as unpredictable in life habits as the northern pike. Anglers have cussed and discussed this fish for years and will undoubtedly continue to do so in the future.

Popularity of northern pike fishing has taken a long time to develop. For many years anglers considered it of secondary importance, hardly worth their efforts. Then gradually, fishermen began to appreciate the sporting potential of the northern because of its fighting spirit, great abundance, and wide distribution. Today, northern pike fishing continues to increase in popularity throughout its range, gaining new enthusiasts each season.

The northern pike is a predacious fish that will eat almost anything that swims. When small, it feeds on crustaceans and insects, but soon switches to a main diet of other fish. As an adult, it is not fussy about food, quantity being more important than quality. Analysis of stomach contents by scientists has revealed that in addition to fish it will at times also take reptiles, frogs, crayfish, mice, young ducks, insects, leeches, and snails.

This varied diet favors the fisherman's use of assorted lures to catch the northern. Bright metal spoons are popular with many anglers, though it has never been fully determined whether the northern hits these spoons thinking they are food, or from anger. Spoon-type lures are often trolled behind a boat, but they can also be cast and retrieved. Either way, the spoon should move moderately fast through the water. Many anglers retrieve or troll with jerks on the rod to vary the speed and action of the spoon. Pike can often be enticed into hitting the lure by this method when other tricks fail. Experimenting is the key to fishing success.

Underwater and surface plugs also attract northern pike. Usually, plugs with plenty of action are good. Wobblers or crippled minnow type plugs bring best results. The color of the plug seems to have little to do with its effectiveness. The color which produces good catches of northerns one day may be totally ignored the next. In fact, the same is true for the type of lure used. Most pike fishermen prefer to take along a

Distribution: Alaska, British Columbia, Labrador, Ohio Valley, Lake Champlain drainage. Eastern South Dakota and Iowa. Introduced in other areas.

Local names: Great northern pike, jackpike, jack, pike, jackfish, pickerel, snake.

Trolling near weeds in a Canadian lake produced a big pike for these anglers

Avoid the northern pike's sharp teeth by using a pair of longnosed pliers to remove the hook lodged in mouth.

tackle box loaded with a variety of artificial lures in various colors and sizes when going after this unpredictable customer.

Anglers often catch northerns while fishing for other species. Walleye fishermen dropping spinners and minnows into a choice hole sometimes find a pike on the end of their line. Bass fishermen using surface plugs are often surprised by a northern leaping clear of the water to hit the plug.

The northern pike is a strong fighter both on top and below the surface of the water. Its strike is usually fast and hard leaving little doubt in the fisherman's mind that he has caught a fish. Sometimes, relatively small northern pike will hit a lure with such force that the angler is convinced he has hooked a very large fish. Again, however, the northern pike is unpredictable. Both large and small pike will occasionally strike a lure and then put forth very little effort in attempting to throw the hook or to escape from the boat.

Bait-casting or spinning tackle are popular with northern pike fishermen. But since large northerns are often hooked, a fairly stiff rod with at least 10-pound test line is the choice of most pike anglers. Spinning tackle, of course, permits the use of lighter lines because of the reel's tension mechanism.

Veteran anglers use a strong leader when fishing specifically for northern pike. Wire leaders, either single strand or braided, are favored by some fishermen, since the many sharp teeth of this fish will easily cut an ordinary fishing line. Good swivels at both ends of the leader prevent the line from twisting as the spoon lure is trolled.

It is not unusual for an angler to spot a northern following a retrieved lure to the boat or shore without striking. Occasionally, a pike will decide to hit a lure just as the fisherman is lifting the lure from the water. This habit often results in a startled, and often splashed, angler caught completely off guard.

Once hooked, the northern will often immediately make a short, strong run in an attempt to throw the hook. At this point, some anglers give the fish a little line but the line should never be allowed to go slack. Fishermen should try to keep a hooked northern away from the boat or shore until it is played out. Even when exhausted, the northern pike's first look at the boat, angler, or shore will usually send it off on another run. After the fish is played out, it must be netted quickly; the pike recovers its strength rapidly. Experienced anglers keep their tackle boxes closed to prevent a flopping northern in the bottom of the boat from scattering lures.

The northern pike generally inhabits the shallower waters of lakes and streams, but in hot weather, it moves to deeper water where it is more difficult to catch. Because this fish feeds constantly, it can be found in waters containing the largest numbers of food fish. The best fishing is usually around weed beds, rocky bars, brush piles, or below rapids or riffles in a stream.

The best time of the year for northern pike fishing comes in the spring and fall when fish inhabit the shallower waters. Some veteran fishermen believe that the northern pike quits hitting lures or bait in the summer because he loses his teeth, but scientists who have studied this theory find it is untrue. Although the northern pike may lose a few teeth from time to time, scientists report that he feeds during some part of each day throughout the summer. Probably one reason fewer fish are caught in hot weather is that the northern seeks the deeper, cooler water where he is more difficult to locate. Also, the warmer water sometimes makes it sluggish.

In some areas, ice fishing for northern pike is legal. Spearing the pike in winter is another method of taking this fish in certain localities, but anglers should check local fishing laws as sportsmen oppose this activity.

Northern pike spawn in the early spring, about the time the ice is going out of lakes and streams. The fish migrate to shallow water and enter small streams or marshy areas to spawn. Several male northern pike may accompany one female during the spawning process. The female deposits the eggs at random on the bottom or on submerged vegetation. Pike do not build nests and do not guard the eggs or young. The fry feed on small water insects and by the end of the first season reach 6 to 8 inches in length.

Hatcheries successfully rear pike for stocking purposes. The northern is sometimes introduced into lakes or streams overpopulated with stunted fish. Because of his voracious appetite, it is hoped that the northern pike will reduce the stunted fish population.

Although somewhat bony, the meat of the northern has good flavor. Though not as highly regarded as some other species of fish, filleting helps to make it excellent to eat.

A boy's thrill in catching a large northern pike will often make him an enthusiastic lifetime fisherman.

A quick field mark for separating the pike family

Pickerel
CHEEK—FULLY SCALED
GILL COVER—FULLY SCALED

Northern pike
CHEEK—FULLY SCALED
GILL COVER—SCALES ON UPPER HALF

Muskellunge
CHEEK—SCALES ON UPPER HALF
GILL COVER—SCALES ON UPPER HALF

Muskellunge

Esox masquinongy

Fishermen probably devote more hours of actual fishing time to the muskellunge, with fewer catches, than to any other fresh-water fish. The muskellunge, or muskie as this fish is commonly known, has a magic appeal for fishermen, and with good reason.

The muskie is one of the largest fresh-water fishes in North America. This, plus his fighting characteristics, is enough to whet the fishing appetites of most anglers. But even more appealing to many fishermen, is the fact that this fresh-water tiger can be very difficult to get on the end of a fishing line.

In numbers, this fish is fairly abundant in the area of its distribution. But the number hooked and boated each year is something else again. Swimming freely, it is a brooding, unpredictable fish that turns into a ferocious fighter once a fisherman is lucky enough to get it to strike.

Many fishermen diligently fish good muskie waters several seasons without catching a

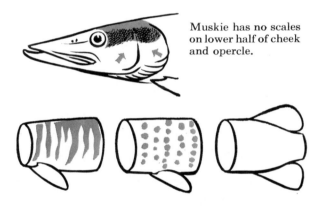

Muskie has no scales on lower half of cheek and opercle.

The body of the muskellunge can be either barred, covered with dark spots, or entirely clear.

muskie of any size. Other fishermen, out after this fish for the first time, will land a real beauty. At times, in waters the muskie generally inhabit, not a fish will be caught for days regardless of the number of devoted fishermen. At other times, such as July, 1955, in Leech Lake, Minnesota, the muskie goes wild. In two days on Leech Lake, 55 of these wary fish were caught. There's no explaining the actions of the muskie, and this is another reason why it is a great sporting fish.

The muskie feeds almost entirely on other fish although it is known also to eat small land animals and birds, such as mice, muskrats, ducks, and grebes. It can be taken, on occasion, with either artificial lures or live bait presented by casting, trolling, or still fishing. Most of these

Distribution: North of St. Lawrence, Ottawa Rivers, through Great Lakes and southern Ontario, western New York, Ohio River Basin, Tennessee River System, Minnesota, and Wisconsin.

Local names: Muskie, lunge, maskinonge.

Barred

Variable markings on muskellunge

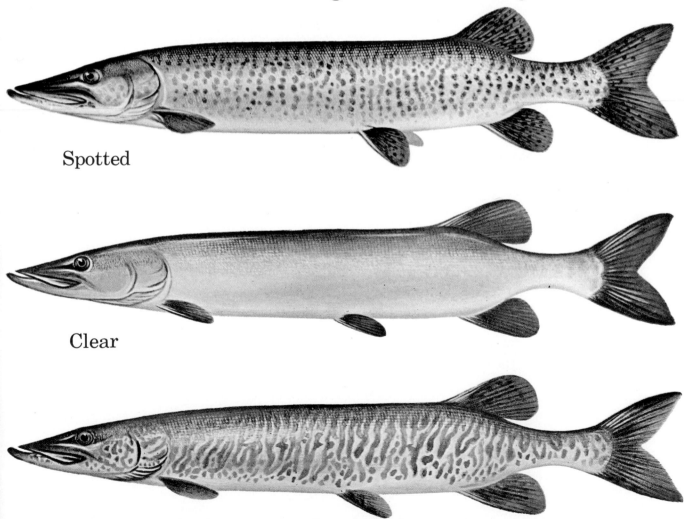

Spotted

Clear

Hybrid (muskellunge—northern pike)

fish are caught by fishermen trolling either live bait or artificial lures, but casting spoons, bucktails, or surface plugs often prove successful when other methods fail.

Even when the muskie doesn't strike, it is a thrill to see this fish follow the lure as it is retrieved, giving the angler a chance to see him come up next to the boat. But it is also a helpless feeling to watch such a beauty slip away with no way of further enticing him to the bait. Experienced fishermen know that once they raise a muskie and miss, they should leave the fish alone for several hours before trying again.

Muskie's solitary habits aid anglers

Muskies stake out a territory on a point of reef or good bay and will stay there for the summer, usually chasing all others from the area. So it is possible to hop from one battler to another in good water, trying your luck in catching one in an ugly or hungry mood. Spoons and spinner bucktail combinations are easier to set the hooks with, but many anglers feel that muskies hit surface plugs more readily.

When hooked, the muskie will usually head for the surface immediately and come out of the water in a shower of spray. It may leap time after time, or it may leap only once and then head for the bottom and sulk.

Landing a big muskie takes time and patience. They are strong fish and must be played carefully so the hook won't be thrown, the line broken, or the hooks pulled out of the mouth. Most fishermen play a muskie until it is tired out before attempting to land it. Even when the fish rolls on its side, completely spent to all appearances, take care when you haul it into the boat. The muskie will undoubtedly muster plenty of fight once it realizes it is out of the water. Some fishermen quiet their catch with a length of pipe or a wooden club.

Angling methods vary with fishermen

The muskie's diet consists almost entirely of fish, some weighing several pounds. Whenever the opportunity presents itself he will attack and eat small land animals and birds.

The most commonly used live bait is a sucker about 12-inches long which can be fished in two ways. Many fishermen simply troll the sucker behind a boat, while others cast the bait fish hour after hour, an effective but arm-wearying business. The other method of using a sucker bait is to still fish. This type of muskie fishing requires a great deal of patience, more than many fishermen possess. The still fishing method using a sucker for bait works best when a muskie is known to be lingering around a point, a sunken log, or a submerged rock pile. They can often be seen lying on or near the bottom in clear water.

When a muskie has been located either by diligent water searching, or by having one strike a lure or bait, resulting in a thrown hook, the still-fishing sucker-bait fisherman can concentrate on that particular fish. The sucker is tossed into the water as close as possible to where the fish is thought to be located, then the fisherman sits back to wait. It may take the muskie three hours or more to decide whether or not he will take the sucker. He may not take it at all regardless of time, or he may take it immediately.

Once it does grab the sucker bait, the fisherman is usually still in for a long wait. The muskie often mouths the sucker but makes no attempt to swallow it, consequently the hook can't be set. It may swim slowly away with the sucker in its mouth but not to the point where the hook can be set. Muskellunge grab food fish in the middle and that is what they do with the sucker. Until he is ready to turn the sucker around head first to be swallowed, all the fisherman can do is wait.

Good muskie fishermen can tell when the muskie has decided to swallow the sucker. The action of the line as it moves through the water is the tip-off. The hook is then set with a strong jerk and the action begins.

How do they differ from northerns?

The life habits of the muskie are similar to those of the northern pike, but the muskie is much more wary and elusive, and spawning occurs considerably later. Also, the muskie on the average will grow to be a larger fish than the northern pike. The world's record muskie weighed almost 70 pounds. Large, record-class muskellunge are over 20 years old.

Muskellunge are found in both rivers and lakes. Spawning takes place in midspring and the eggs are deposited by the female as she slowly swims through shallow water. The male swims alongside and fertilizes the eggs as they fall to the bottom.

The eggs, left unattended, hatch in about two weeks. Many of the newly hatched muskellunge are eaten by northern pike or larger muskies. Muskellunge are now being produced with varying degrees of success by fish hatcheries for stocking in lakes and rivers.

Solitude vanishes as a muskie explodes into action from his dark hiding place →

Grass pickerel

Esox americanus vermiculatus

Distribution: From southern Wisconsin to the St. Lawrence River and Lake Champlain and south. West to Gulf Coast of Alabama and Texas.

Local names: Mud pickerel, little pickerel, redfin pickerel.

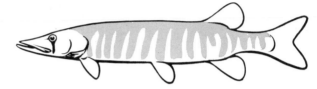

The body of the grass pickerel is usually vertically barred or mottled with dark color.

Both cheek and opercle fully scaled, black tear drop below eye almost vertical, snout concave; longer.

Distribution: Saint Lawrence River and south near Atlantic Coast to Florida.

Local names: Banded pickerel, barred pickerel.

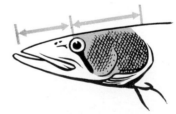

Cheek and opercle fully scaled. Oblique black tear drop below eye. Snout usually convex, shorter from tip to eye than eye to back of head.

Redfin pickerel

Esox americanus americanus

Chain pickerel

Esox niger

Of the three pickerel found in North America, only the chain pickerel is of particular interest to fishermen. The other two, the grass pickerel and the redfin pickerel, rarely attain a size that interests many anglers.

All three of the pickerel have similar life histories. These fish prefer shallow water and usually inhabit the weedy sections of a lake. A few pickerel live in small, slow-moving tributary streams but this fish is primarily found in lakes and ponds.

The chain pickerel will usually average two to three pounds in weight, but occasionally one will exceed 5 pounds. The grass pickerel runs 8 to 13 inches in length, the redfin pickerel rarely exceeds 12 inches.

Either of these pickerel can be taken with hook and line but the redfin and the grass pickerel are seldom fished for, due to their small size. The chain pickerel is a popular sporting fish, however, and many fishermen eagerly try their skill on this game fighter. Some anglers claim that the chain pickerel will make more jumps before coming to the net than any other member of the pike family. In eastern United States, pickerel fishing is prime sport, but farther south the enthusiasm slackens because of intense in-

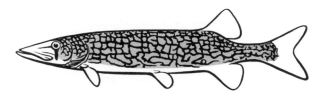

Dark chain-like markings on body and head. Generally yellow-olive with white belly. Largest of pickerel.

Both cheek and opercle fully scaled. Black tear drop below eye, almost vertical.

terest in largemouth bass and bluegill fishing.

Pickerel feed almost exclusively on small fish, but they readily hit artificial lures, especially spoons. On a fly rod, using streamer flies or small spinner lures, the chain pickerel can be a worthy adversary. In many areas, fishing through the ice for pickerel is a popular method of catching this fish. According to fishery records, many more pickerel are taken through the ice than are caught by summer fishermen. The pickerel feeds all year long, during both day and night.

The spawning habits of the pickerel are similar to those of the northern pike and muskellunge. Eggs laid in shallow water and left unattended hatch in about two weeks. The young pickerel feed primarily on insects until they reach about six inches in length then switch their diet to small fish.

The meat of the pickerel is good, but many small bones make these fish less popular than other species.

Distribution: Nova Scotia, New Brunswick, Quebec, south across the eastern United States to Florida, west to Texas, Mississippi Valley north to Missouri.

Local names: Pike, river pike, grass pike, jack, jackfish.

Minnow and sucker families

Any small fish is often referred to as a minnow; however, such terminology is incorrect as minnows belong to a specific family. Of the nearly 200 American species in this family, a few like carp, squawfish, and fallfish reach a size to be of interest to sport fishermen. Squawfish, for instance, occasionally weigh up to 80 pounds. In some areas, smaller species of minnows are propagated artificially for bait.

Minnows are found in all types of water from sea level streams to high altitude lakes, many times tolerating water other fish are unable to inhabit. They serve as an important food source for a great many fresh-water game fish.

Like the minnow, though generally classified among the rough fishes, the sucker gains in popularity in areas where major game fish are scarce. The few species large enough to provide sport will give a good tussle when taken on light tackle. Sucker fishing in some areas of the South is so important that private hatcheries have been established for propagation.

Seining "rough" fish out of a lake

← In some areas, carp and suckers are considered rough or trash fish and are destroyed. Fishermen in other areas where game fish are scarce welcome the opportunity to fish for these species. Chemical poisoning of lakes and streams to rid them of so-called trash fish remains a debatable practice. Game fish are sometimes killed; long-term effects are unknown.

Peamouth

Mylocheilus caurinus

Peamouth has small mouth, barbel, red area at jaw angle.

Each side has two dark stripes. Dorsal and anal fins, 8 rays.

Golden shiner

Notemigonus crysoleucas

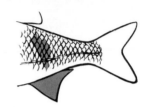

Anal fin long, sail-shaped. Scales are large, conspicuous.

Lateral line curves sharply downward. Mouth curves up.

Creek chub

Semotilus atromaculatus

Mouth large and oblique; groove between lip and snout.

Spot on dorsal. Front of dorsal behind front of pelvic fin.

Fallfish

Semotilus corporalis

Mouth large, upper jaw barbel; dark spot behind head.

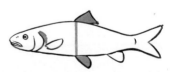

No spot on dorsal fin. Pelvic fin vertical to dorsal fin.

Distribution: Columbia River and tributaries, British Columbia, coastal streams of Oregon and Washington.

Local names: Whitefish, Columbia chub.

The peamouth, found in both rivers and lakes, may grow to 12 inches in length but averages much smaller. It is unpopular with most fishermen although it can be caught on hook and line with either bait or flies. The meat is bony and not particularly good to eat.

This member of the minnow family maintains a diet of insects and small crustaceans. Its value lies primarily in serving as food for trout, salmon, and other species.

Distribution: Occurs in eastern half of United States and southern Canada, Nova Scotia to Manitoba, south to Oklahoma, Texas and Florida.

Local names: Shiner, American roach, dace, chub.

This minnow is a fish of ponds, lakes, and sluggish streams. In lakes, the golden shiner may reach a length of 12 or more inches, though the average fish runs 3 to 4 inches. It feeds on plankton, insects, snails, and occasionally small fish. Shiners are an important food for other species of fish and are raised commercially for bait.

Few anglers fish for the golden shiner intentionally. Youngsters can have a good deal of fun still fishing for this minnow using very small hooks and dough baits.

Distribution: Nova Scotia, Great Lakes System, west across the United States to Montana, south to New Mexico, east to northern Florida, Georgia and Gulf States.

Local names: Chub, horned dace, common chub, northern creek chub.

The creek chub rarely reaches a length of more than 10 inches, but it is a sporty little fish when taken on a fly rod. Some states permit year-around fishing for this minnow which is good to eat and fun to catch.

As a bait fish, the creek chub is hard to beat. It is hardy and stays alive in a minnow bucket longer than most species. This minnow feeds on insects, crayfish, and small fish and in turn serves as a food supply for many species of game fish.

Distribution: From the James Bay drainage, across eastern Canada, south to Virginia, east side of the mountains.

Local names: Chub, dace, silver chub, white chub, corporal.

The fallfish puts up a good battle for his size and is often caught by anglers fishing for trout. He will rise to a fly and can also be taken on bait. Most fallfish are caught in streams, but they also inhabit lakes.

Insects, worms, crayfish, and small fish make up his diet. A worm on a small hook is a good bait. Adults may reach 12 to 18 inches in length but the average fish runs 6 to 12 inches. Caught in the spring in cold, fast moving streams, these small fish are good to eat.

Carp

Cyprinus carpio

This brawny fish originated in Asia, found its way to Europe and from there was introduced into North America only about 100 years ago. It is prolific and has taken over many quiet waters, often driving out other game fish.

The carp often pollutes the water during feeding by disturbing the bottom while grubbing for tender roots and shoots of young aquatic plants. Species requiring clear water may not thrive around large numbers of carp. Along the same line, however, carp can live in water unsuited for other fish and therefore provide the only fishing available to some anglers.

An omnivorous feeder, the controversial carp includes both vegetable and animal matter in his diet. Dough baits are used extensively in carp fishing, as are worms, minnows, and even corn. Once hooked the carp fights a strong, dogged battle which requires husky tackle. Carp weighing 15 to 20 pounds are not uncommon.

Northern squawfish

Ptychocheilus oregonensis

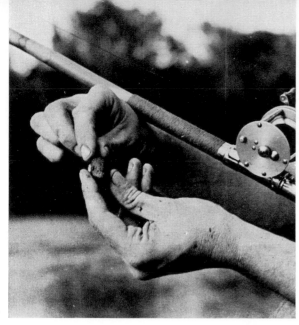

A small hook buried in a dough ball or a ball of corn meal or oatmeal makes excellent bait. Worms, minnows, even kernels of sweet corn are good carp baits.

Though the eating quality of the carp remains controversial, there's no doubt it's a heavy fighter. This angler carries tackle and bait in his basket creel.

Distribution: Native to Asia, brought to America 100 years ago from Europe and presently distributed throughout United States, and parts of southern Canada.

Local names: German carp, scaled carp, mirror carp, leather carp.

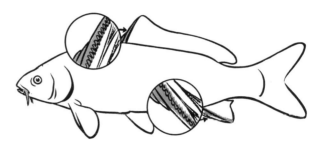

Carp have four barbels, the upper jaw having a pair on each side of the mouth. Body color varies from gold to olive; serrated spine on dorsal, anal fins.

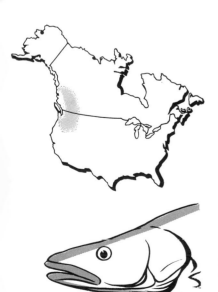

Distribution: Columbia River System; streams north to British Columbia.

Local names: Columbia River squawfish, yellowbelly, bigmouth.

The head of the northern squawfish is long and tapered. Fish has a large mouth, small eye.

Though the northern squawfish is often blamed for the depletion of salmon and trout in some Western rivers, it makes up for its predacious nature by serving in turn as food for other species. Its diet often consists of insects; when food is plentiful, schools of squawfish can often be seen feeding at the surface.

It's not a strong fighter when hooked. However, taken on a fly rod the squawfish will put up a short battle. Its flesh is moderately good to eat, but is filled with small bones.

The Sacramento squawfish, occurring in California and southern Oregon, has a life cycle similar to that of its northern brother. The Colorado squawfish inhabits the Colorado River System, reaching up to 5 feet long to qualify as North America's largest minnow.

Quillback

Carpiodes cyprinus

Distribution: Mississippi River System, lower Great Lakes, Susquehanna River drainage.

Local names: White carp, carpsucker, silver carp, white sucker.

The quillback is not of particular importance to the fisherman, yet many are taken in lakes and streams by anglers in search of other species. In some areas a few fishermen do fish for the quillback because it's edible and provides fair sport on light tackle. Mature fish range around 3 pounds in weight.

This scavenger feeds from the bottom, sucking up plant materials and insect larvae. Common baits used for quillback include grubs, doughballs, and small worms.

Quillback's long rays on the dorsal fin are sometimes broken. Dorsal rays number about 24.

Small sucker mouth. Body cross section is deep and slab-sided.

Northern redhorse

Moxostoma macrolepidotum

Lower fins and tail of northern redhorse are red and orange. Dorsal rays usually 14.

The northern redhorse, taken in large numbers by commercial fishermen, is very good to eat. This fish attracts more attention among anglers, especially during the spawning season in the early spring, than does the quillback.

The most common baits used to catch this bottom feeder are worms, grasshoppers, grubs, or small pieces of meat. The best place to fish is in the current or gravel riffles, much the same as for channel catfish.

Sucker mouth with ridges on lips. Body cross section almost cylindrical.

Distribution: South Central, eastern Canada, New York west to Montana, Kansas.

Local names: Redfin, redfin sucker, bigscale sucker, mullet.

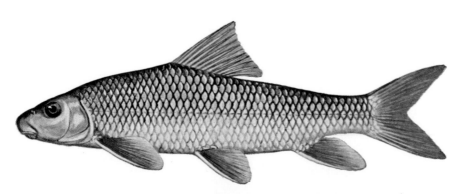

White sucker

Catostomus commersoni

Due to its abundance, the white sucker is taken in large numbers each year by both commercial and sport fishermen. Although bony, it is very good to eat. It averages around 16 inches in length and is a tough fighter when taken on light tackle.

Fishing for suckers as they migrate to spawn is great sport in some areas. White suckers usu-

Smaller scales than redhorse with scales crowded forward on body. Dorsal fin rays 11 or 12.

Sucker mouth with papillae on lips. Body cross section almost cylindrical.

Distribution: Eastern Canada, Northwest Territories, south to New Mexico.

Local names: Sucker, blacksucker, common sucker, mullet.

ally inhabit the deeper pools in a stream, but also can be caught around sunken logs, brush piles, and immediately below riffles.

These fish will occasionally hit wet flies fished near the bottom and many have been caught on spinning lures. Common baits include those used for quillback and redhorse.

Fishing for suckers

Floating small streams with a canoe is an excellent way to fish for the white sucker. The best time of the year to fish is probably during the spring spawning migration.

This method of fishing eliminates long walks from one productive spot to the next. The angler reaches areas not easily accessible by car or walking, and avoids over-fished spots near roads and bridges.

Maynard Reece

Catfish family

Probably no other family of fishes has more disparaging remarks made about it than does the catfish family. Nonetheless millions of pounds of these fish are caught and eaten every year by dedicated catfish fishermen.

In the Midwest more bullheads are caught than all other fish combined. Families make fishing trips into all-night parties with dozens of fish boated and kept for the table. Catfish are also important for commercial markets.

The appearance of the catfish—scaleless, wide mouthed, with whiskerlike sensory barbels on the upper and lower jaw—may be one reason why it receives more than its share of comments. While obviously not a handsome fish it is relatively easy to catch and excellent on the dinner table.

The catfish family has an effective defense mechanism—sharp pectoral and dorsal spines that can be held stiffly erect. In some species these spines are serrated, in others they are coated with venom. A careless angler can be stuck with these spines causing a painful, though harmless, wound. All the catfish family can be eaten safely.

These bottom feeders live in either clean or muddy water. It is not uncommon to find them in polluted water that would kill other species.

The driftwood home of channel catfish

←Since fallen trees and woodpiles are choice spots of catfish these are two places for the angler to try his skill. Snags and the ease with which Mr. Whiskers can wrap a line around a log make losing both catfish and fishing tackle part of the sport.

Channel catfish

Ictalurus punctatus

To many a veteran angler there's no better catch than a "mess of channel cats." Whether it's the fun of catching these fish, or the joy of eating them, channel catfish rate high with a large number of fishermen.

The channel catfish prefers the larger rivers or lowland lakes, but will stay in deep holes in fairly small streams. It is not as large a fish as some of the other species of catfish. The average fish taken by anglers usually runs about a foot in length, though specimens of 10 to 25 pounds or more are sometimes caught.

Like other members of its family, the channel catfish has a varied appetite. It feeds on insects, vegetation, and other fish, both dead and alive. Though it eats an assortment of food, this fish feeds exclusively on a particular item at certain seasons. When the elm tree seeds are falling whole schools of channel cat often gorge themselves on this one food.

Spawning occurs in summer when the water temperature reaches 75 degrees, with the eggs deposited in such secluded places as rock ledges, holes, cutouts in the river bank, logs, even in

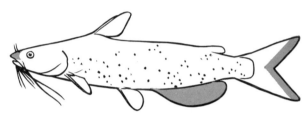

Upper jaw longer than lower, tail deeply forked. Body usually spotted, anal fin rounded with 24 to 30 rays. All the catfish family have smooth skin, 8 barbels.

man-made objects such as tin cans and drainage tile. A female catfish around 4 pounds will lay 3,000 to 8,000 eggs. Once spawning takes place the male drives the female away from the nest and guards the eggs for ten days or so until they hatch. The fry travel in schools.

Catfish can be caught by a variety of methods. Still fishing the deeper holes or areas around log jams and sunken debris in a river or lake is often productive. The angler should be quiet and keep as far away from the spot as possible to avoid spooking this sensitive fish.

The catfish often prefers fast-moving water. A favorite fishing spot for many anglers is the area directly below a river dam where the channel cat waits for food to be washed to it. Though this long-whiskered fellow is primarily a bottom feeder, float fishing in rivers—using a bobber and light sinker to keep the bait just below the surface as it floats with the current—is effective.

Almost any type of fishing tackle can be used for catching channel catfish. Many anglers favor hand lines, cane poles, or a 7-foot Calcutta pole, while others prefer casting or spinning tackle with a heavy action.

Distribution: From southern Canada and Great Lakes south in Mississippi and Colorado River System to Mexico. Atlantic coast, Florida north to Virginia.

Local names: Spotted cat, fiddler, Great Lakes catfish.

Many kinds of bait take catfish. Dough baits, chicken entrails, coagulated chicken blood, worms, shrimp, crayfish, or frogs at one time or another produce good catches. Small minnows, both live and dead, are the favorite bait of many fishermen. In the fall this catfish will often hit artificial lures when cast up and across the current and retrieved in erratic jerks as the bait drifts downstream. Some anglers present an artificial lure, often some type of jig, by slowly bumping it along the bottom of the stream.

The channel catfish feeds primarily at night. For this reason, nighttime fishing is usually more productive than fishing during the daylight hours. It will feed in the channels and deep water during the twilight hours, moving into the shallows at dark. The exception and best time of all to catch catfish is on sudden rises of the river or stream. No matter what time of day, experienced anglers fish the instant the water starts to rise and continue for the next few hours. If the rise occurs during daylight hours, they fish around deep holes, under banks, and near brush piles. Temperature of the water also affects catfish angling. If the water becomes cold, catfish are slow to bite.

The channel cat adapts well to stocking in ponds either alone or in combination with bass, bluegills, or crappies. It has done much to increase the popularity of catfish fishing.

This angler fishes a typical channel catfish hole on the Des Moines River using a 7-foot Calcutta pole and reel.

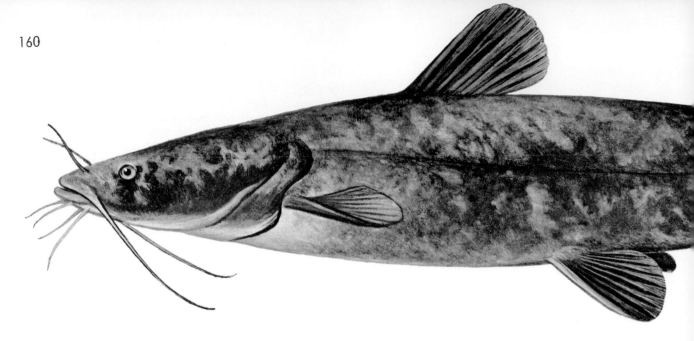

Flathead catfish

Pylodictis olivaris

It is always a good idea to use heavy tackle when fishing for the flathead catfish. Specimens weighing as much as 100 pounds have been taken from rivers across the country. Three- to four-pound fish are more commonly caught by fresh-water fishermen but 20 to 40 pound flatheads are not unusual.

Almost any kind of bait can be used to catch this catfish. The flathead, like other members of its family, feeds on most any food it can locate and catch. A catfish's highly developed senses allow it to feed by touch, taste, and smell, as well as by sight. For this reason they are taken in muddy water which normally would not produce fish which feed primarily by sight. Under turbid conditions baits that have a strong odor are highly effective.

Baits favored among veteran anglers include cheese, chicken entrails, congealed blood, big mass of worms, or a good-sized chub. Softer baits are sometimes encased in fine netting to keep them from disintegrating in the water.

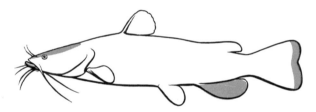

The head is flattened between the eyes. The lower jaw is longer than the upper jaw. Tail is slightly notched; anal fin has about 16 rays.

The flathead feeds primarily at night, often swimming into the shallows in search of food. These areas produce good fishing after dark.

The flathead catfish is primarily a bottom feeder so present the bait to him on or near the river floor. Still fishing ranks high as the favorite method of angling for the flathead, but some fishermen will slowly retrieve their bait, bumping it along the bottom, hoping to entice the fish to take it.

Most anglers learn early not to set the hook when the flathead first jerks on their line; he may mouth the bait for some time before finally deciding to swallow it. Premature attempts to set the hook will invariably end in failure and an immediate loss of the evening's best customer.

Contrary to what many fishermen believe, this fish has been caught on such artificial lures as spoons and lead-head jigs retrieved along the bottom. Flatheads are strong fighters.

Distribution: South Dakota to Pennsylvania, south to Mississippi Valley to the gulf. Rio Grande in Mexico.

Local names: Shovelhead cat, mud cat.

Whether large or small the flathead catfish is a worthy adversary for any fisherman. It takes heavy tackle, strong arms, and cool patience to land a 20- to 40-pound specimen. His appearance may not be the most handsome, but once on the table, this fellow is mighty good to eat.

White catfish

Ictalurus catus

At maturity, the white catfish isn't as large as his flathead brother, but averages about 12 inches in length and weighs 2 or 3 pounds; maximum size pushes 14 pounds.

It's a good idea to use a fairly stiff rod and strong line for white catfish, not because of its weight as much as its habitat. Underwater roots, log jams, sunken debris are favorite spots for most catfish. Fishermen usually find they spend a good deal of time freeing snagged lines or keeping a tight line on a fish trying to reach a driftwood pile as it struggles for freedom.

Distribution: In rivers draining into Atlantic from Hudson River south to Florida. Also introduced in many Western states.

Local names: None

Upper jaw is longer than lower jaw, no spots on body. White catfish has a moderately forked tail, the anal fin is rounded with 18-24 rays.

Blue catfish

Ictalurus furcatus

The blue catfish, weighing sometimes more than 100 pounds, is the largest member of the catfish family. Specimens weighing 25 pounds or more are frequently caught by hook-and-line fishermen, but it takes stout tackle and strong arms to land one of these stubborn fighters.

This heavyweight is found in the larger rivers or the mouths of streams flowing into large rivers. The blue cat is hardy and has been successfully stocked in a great many artificial ponds, lakes, and impoundments. It will eat everything it can find or catch, therefore, as with other members of its family, the fisherman has a wide choice of baits.

In addition to favorite catfish habitats, the blue catfish is found in the deep holes below some dams and spillways. Like the channel cat, it often inhabits fairly fast-moving water as well as slow-moving portions of a river. Spawning occurs in spring when water temperature reaches 70 to 75 degrees. The male guards eggs and fry.

The temperature of water has an effect upon the catfish's feeding habits as its body temperature varies with its environment. It is generally correct to say that these fish will feed more when the water temperature is above 70 degrees, than when it is below 50 degrees. An exception to this statement occurs during the summer spawning period when the male feeds very little due to the demand of his domestic tasks. Another exception is in late fall when declining water temperatures seem to stimulate the catfish's appetite as long as the water remains above 40 degrees during at least part of the day. Once the water temperature stays below 40 degrees, feeding drops off rapidly.

The blue and channel catfish are often mistaken for one another. Each has a deeply forked caudal fin and an upper jaw longer than the lower jaw. To complicate identification, during spawning season the male channel cat changes from its normal silver gray to a bluish hue. Result is that many of the "blue" catfish caught in summer are really channel cats in spawning color.

The blue catfish, like other members of its family, is cleaned by skinning.

Check anal fin to distinguish between blue catfish and male channel cat which turns blue during spawning.

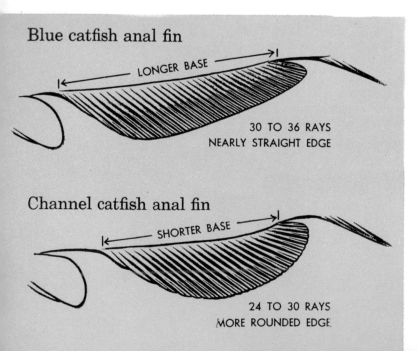

Blue catfish anal fin

LONGER BASE

30 TO 36 RAYS
NEARLY STRAIGHT EDGE

Channel catfish anal fin

SHORTER BASE

24 TO 30 RAYS
MORE ROUNDED EDGE

Distribution: Mississippi River System and other Gulf Coastal rivers.

Local names: Fork-tail cat, great blue cat, chucklehead cat.

Upper jaw is longer than lower. The tail is deeply forked. Blue catfish has no spots on body or tail. The anal fin is straight-edged with 30 to 36 rays.

This angler hooked a prize blue catfish by fishing the tail water of a large dam

Brown bullhead

Ictalurus nebulosus

Chin barbels on the brown bullhead are dark. Barbs or spines are present on the back edge of the pectoral fin spine.

Body is usually mottled. Tail is square or slightly notched. Anal fin is gently rounded, has 20-24 rays.

Yellow bullhead

Ictalurus natalis

Chin barbels are whitish or cream-colored. Dorsal area dark olive-brown to yellow, belly is white to yellow.

Tail of this bullhead is rounded and anal fin is straight with dark color along edge. Anal fin has 24 to 29 rays.

Black bullhead

Ictalurus melas

Chin barbels on the black bullhead are dark. The pectoral fin spine is not barbed behind.

Tail slightly notched, whitish bar at base. Anal fin gray at base, rounded, 17-22 rays.

Distribution: Great Lakes and Mississippi drainage system. West to Montana.

Local names: Yellow-belly bullhead.

Hold a bullhead with caution

This angler grips the bullhead carefully to avoid → pricking himself on the dorsal and pectoral spines. These spines have a poisonous gland that coats them, causing pain to punctured skin.

Distribution: Southern Canada, Great Lakes, St. Lawrence south to Florida, west to Mississippi River.

Local names: Common bullhead, speckled bullhead, mud pout, horned pout.

Distribution: From North Dakota to the Great Lakes and St. Lawrence drainages. South to Oklahoma, Texas, and Atlantic Coast.

Local names: Bullhead, yellow-belly bullhead.

The first angling experience for many fishermen was probably dunking a hook and worm in a stream or pond for bullheads. These smaller species of the catfish family, abundant over a wide area of North America, are often considered the favorite fish of youngsters and experienced fishermen alike.

Bullheads are not famous for their fighting ability though they are scrappy for their size. These scaleless fish win friends with their willingness to take a bait which makes them an excellent sport fish for youngsters inclined to be short on patience.

The different species of bullheads are very similar in life habits. These fish will feed on almost any type of bottom food; insects, worms, insect larvae, small fish, and crustaceans are their primary diet. Worms top the list of baits used by bullhead fishermen. Experienced anglers are generous when stringing worms on a hook. Most fishermen soon learn that a wad of worms is more effective than a single threaded one. A few loose loops of worm should be left dangling from the hook.

Almost any type of tackle serves for bullhead fishing; casting rod, spinning rod, fly rod, or just a cane pole will do. All that is really needed is a hand line with a hook on the end. Regardless of the tackle or bait used, the hook must be fished on or near the bottom of a lake or stream.

Technique for bullhead fishing

Bullheads ordinarily strike by first feeding at the bait, producing short jerks on the line. If the angler uses a float, he sets the hook when the float disappears under the surface of the water or begins to move slowly across the surface. At this time, the bullhead usually has the baited hook in its mouth. Without a float, the hook should be set when the jerks on the line are rapid and strong.

When fishing a lake for bullheads, fishermen often move the boat slowly, using a bobber to keep their bait just off the bottom. Once they catch several bullheads in one spot, the boat is anchored. There's no use moving farther with a school of bullheads swimming around just below them. Quite often the same spot will produce bullheads day after day. As with the rest of the catfish family, night fishing for this species is particularly productive.

Inexperienced anglers should be careful of the sharp spines on the bullhead's dorsal and pectoral fins. The sting of these spines is painful, but not dangerous. Bullheads taken from clear, cold water have excellent flavor.

Bass family

Members of the sea bass family, which includes many salt-water species, primarily inhabit tropical and subtropical waters. The four species of concern to fresh-water fishermen are white bass, yellow bass, white perch, and striped bass.

Of the four fish, white bass and yellow bass are found only in fresh water and average around a pound in weight. The white perch and striped bass commonly spend the major portion of their life cycles in salt or brackish water, but these fish may spawn in fresh-water tributary streams, at which time they are available to fresh-water anglers. When landlocked either naturally or transplanted, both fish can live and reproduce in fresh water without running to the sea.

All four of the fresh-water representatives of the sea bass family are worth a fisherman's time and efforts. They have good fighting characteristics when taken on light tackle. These four species are not particularly temperamental fish and can be caught with either live bait or lures. They make tasty table fare that can be cooked in a variety of ways.

Many anglers expecting to find the smallmouth bass and largemouth bass in this family may be confused by their omission. Taxonomists have proved, however, that these "bass" are members of the sunfish family.

A catch of white bass gleaming in the sun

← This is one of the most plentiful fish found in Southern waters where they are literally caught by the hundreds. Not only is this bass a good fighter, but it stays in large schools affording ample opportunity to fill a stringer rapidly when they are hitting. Though bony, they make tasty fillets.

White bass

Roccus chrysops

Morning or evening is usually the best time to fish for the scrappy white bass. At these times they move into quiet, shallower water or close to the surface to feed. During the middle of the day, white bass prefer deeper water around rocks, sand bars, vegetation, and they can be caught by trolling a spinner-minnow combination near the bottom.

White bass inhabit both lakes and streams. Good catches are often made in moderately fast waters below dams, or at the mouths of tributary streams. The fry feed on insects and their larvae while other fish make up the primary diet of adult white bass. For this reason a majority of fishermen favor minnows as bait; however, lures and dry flies are effective at certain times.

The white bass is easily transplanted and is a favorite fish for stocking reservoirs and artificial

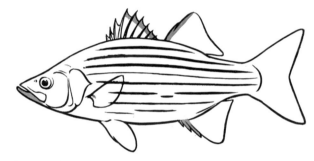

Dorsal fin not joined. Lower jaw projects, dark stripes along body. Teeth on tongue. Anal spines evenly graduated, second spine much shorter than third spine.

ponds in many parts of the country. It is a good fighter and excellent on the table. Maximum weight runs to 5 pounds. Filleting is the fastest and easiest method of cleaning this bass.

In many of the large impoundments in the South, white bass make up a high percentage of the fish caught for food. Since it is one fish that can increase and crowd out all other species in a short time, most fish commissions have liberal or no restrictions on numbers taken. Fishing from docks and piers at night under lights is popular. After a night's "work" some eager fishermen take home as many as 500 white bass to fillet. This may appear to be poor conservation but most authorities agree that this species is a short-lived fast-growing fish and should be harvested accordingly.

Distribution: Great Lakes and Mississippi River drainages. Stocked in many other areas.

Local names: barfish, stripers, silver bass, striped bass.

This fisherman has located a school of white bass →

Yellow bass

Roccus mississippiensis

The yellow bass is similar to the white bass in its habits and life history. But for fishermen, there is a significant difference between the two which has a direct effect on fishing success. The yellow bass, unlike the white bass, is primarily a deep feeder. This means that the angler must get his bait down to the fish to be effective.

Worms, live minnows, and artificial lures are all effective for yellow bass. Veteran anglers troll until a bass is caught, then drop anchor and still fish. Since the yellow bass travels in schools, others are usually near by.

Dorsal fins joined. Lower jaw nearly even with upper jaw. Dark stripes often broken along deep body. No teeth on tongue. Anal spines not evenly graduated, second and third nearly equal in length.

Spring is the best season for catching yellow bass, with fall a close second choice. There are periods when they will move into shallow water making them prime targets for dry flies, streamers, and small lures. Maximum size is about one pound. Local fishermen often prefer the flavor of yellow bass over that of the white bass.

Distribution: Southern Indiana, Wisconsin, and Minnesota, south to Alabama, Texas, Louisiana, and Oklahoma.

Local names: barfish, yellow perch.

White perch

Roccus americanus

The white perch is a favorite pan fish along the Atlantic coast. Found in schools of hundreds, it is easy to catch. In spring fishermen line the banks of streams and rivers when this fish is running up tributary waters to spawn. An adult fish weighs up to a pound and averages 8 to 12 inches in length.

The white perch doesn't wander far from sea, preferring the brackish waters of ponds connecting to the sea or the brackish waters of bays and river mouths. However, it appears to do better than most anadromous fish (species living in salt water that enter rivers to spawn) for it thrives in strictly fresh water and can reproduce there with no migration to the ocean.

This fish feeds on all kinds of fry, shrimp, crabs, and the spawn of other fishes. In fresh water, the white perch feeds on water fleas, minnows, nymphs, and insect larvae.

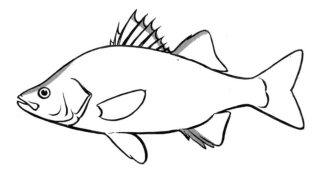

Dorsal fins joined, top of head concave. No teeth on tongue. No stripes; anal spines not evenly graduated.

Live bait is used extensively for catching white perch. Worms and minnows are favorites; small pieces of crab are also effective. Many anglers use very small spinning lures, while fly-fishing enthusiasts prefer bucktails, tiny wet flies, or spinners.

In fresh water, fish for white perch in a sandy, clean bottom at depths from 10 to 20 feet. At times, these fish also congregate in shallow areas in search of minnows.

The white perch spawns in spring and early summer. The eggs are distributed on the stream bottom and left without care or guarding by the parents. With water temperature at 60° the eggs hatch in about 2 days.

The Chesapeake Bay area and all the tributary streams of that region contain heavy concentrations of white perch. It is important commercially as well as a fine sport fish for hook and line fishermen. White perch are considered exceptionally good to eat.

Distribution: Eastern Canada from Gulf of St. Lawrence to Nova Scotia. In eastern United States from Lakes Erie and Ontario to Atlantic Coast south to the Carolinas.

Local names: Bluenose perch, gray perch, sea perch.

Striped bass

Roccus saxatilis

Until recent years, striped bass were strictly coastal fish, running into fresh-water streams to spawn. Normally, this fish is found where the surf runs high, in tidal rips, bays, and brackish waters. Recently, however, transplants of striped bass have been made into landlocked fresh-water lakes in the South and West coast.

Despite the failure of some transplants, others are successful and demonstrate that the striped bass can reproduce without spending part of its life in salt water. Proof of this comes from the Kerr Reservoir shared by North Carolina and Virginia. In 1953, a million fry were transferred here from the Weldon, North Carolina, hatchery with an additional two million added later.

By 1955 fishermen started catching small stripers while fishing for crappies. They are now catching up to 12-pound fish, with test nets picking up fry although no fry have been stocked in later years, thus indicating that the fish can complete their life cycle cut off from salt water. Arkansas, Kentucky, and Tennessee have stocked various areas.

Although the striped bass was originally found only in Atlantic and Gulf coastal waters,

Dorsal fins not joined, top of head convex, teeth on tongue. Dark stripes on body. Much larger and slimmer than other basses. Lower jaw is longer than upper.

transplants to the waters of the Pacific coast have been successful. It is now an important game fish of that area. Commercial netting of striped bass, which was once a big business, is no longer permitted by many states.

The weight of striped bass caught by fishermen varies from 3 to 40 pounds. However, fish weighing over 100 pounds have been recorded in salt water. Most of these were caught many years ago. A 65-pounder is a very large fish today. Fresh-water stripers usually run in the 5- to 10-pound class.

Striped bass can be taken with a variety of artificial lures as well as live bait. Many people still fish with large minnows. Others will troll until one hits and then stop to fish for others in the school. Jigs and heavy spoons are favorite lures. Stripers hit hard and are good fighters. Heavy tackle is generally used since in many impoundments there is much flooded brush and trees to tangle gear. These fish are excellent as food and can be served in a variety of ways.

Distribution: Atlantic and Pacific coastal waters, lakes in South and West.

Local names: Striper, rockfish.

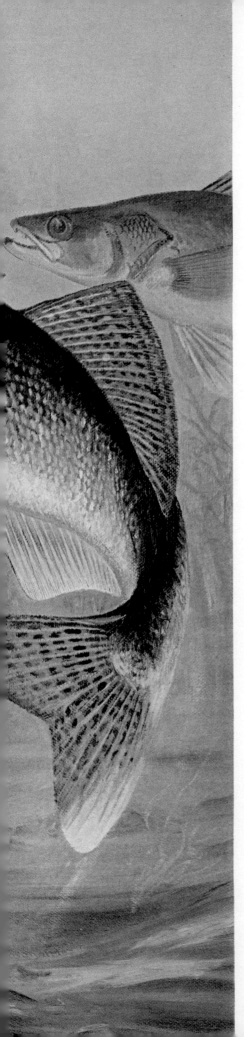

Perch family

Although there are 100 species of fish in the perch family, only 3 are of interest to sport fishermen—the walleye, sauger, and yellow perch. These fish, however, are among the most important sport fish in North America. From the boy who has just caught his first yellow perch on a bamboo pole to the experienced angler carefully landing a 10-pound walleye, the fishing public has a firm respect for this family.

These three species are widely distributed throughout lakes and streams in the United States and Canada. They strike equally well on artificial and live bait, which accounts in part for their popularity. By taking advantage of their habit to school, an angler can often fill his stringer once he has located one fish and found a bait that will produce a strike. Though these 3 fish are not the top fighters of the fish kingdom, they do have enough underwater strength to put up a good fight on light tackle. The flavor of their meat is excellent.

The other species in the perch family, which are of little interest to fishermen, are called darters, receiving their name from an ability to move and stop quickly. Darters seldom exceed 2½ to 3 inches in length, but rank among the most colorful fresh-water species. They are known as bottom fish and inhabit fast-moving streams, weed beds of lakes, or sand bars of rivers where they are seldom visible to fishermen.

Walleye, largest member of the perch family

← The large, opaque eyes of this fish give it the name, walleye. They travel in schools and prefer cold water with a sand, gravel, or rocky bottom. When an angler catches one walleye, he's likely to catch more in the same spot. These fish are predators with big appetites and they play an important part in maintaining the fish balances in large, open-water lakes.

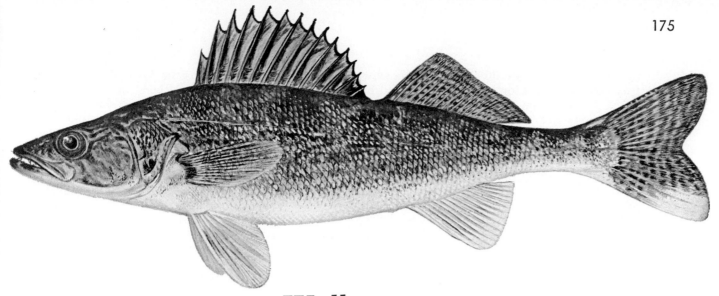

Walleye

Stizostedion vitreum vitreum

Thousands of fishermen would rather catch their limits of walleyes than any other fish. The walleye is excellent to eat and is distributed widely in North America. In addition, it is a respectable fighter when taken on hook and line.

Walleyes are most numerous in large, open-water lakes with sand and gravel bottoms but many are caught in streams and rivers. They can be taken by several methods using a variety of artificial lures and live baits. The average size for walleye is 1½ to 3 pounds. However, 5-pound fish are not uncommon and the world's record fish weighs just under 24 pounds.

Trolling for walleyes with artificial lures or minnow-spinner combinations is popular in many areas. The boat speed should be kept fairly slow for best results, slower than when trolling for northern pike, for instance.

Walleyes travel in loose schools and where one is caught a fisherman can be reasonably sure

The walleye has a black blotch in back part of first or spinous dorsal fin, a white tip on the lower lobe of the tail. Strong teeth and opaque eyes.

of catching others. Many anglers troll back and forth across sand bars or drop offs until they take the first fish. A marker is then thrown out of the boat and trolling is continued around that spot. The practice of leaving a marker in a lake is illegal in some states. A better method is to line up landmarks on shore so imaginary lines from these points bisect the choice spot on the lake. This method not only marks the same spot that day but enables the fisherman to return to the area on later trips.

Walleyes often lie along the edges of sand bars or drop offs. Here, they move slowly back and forth waiting for food to be washed to them or for an unwary school of minnows or other small fish to swim past. They can also be found at the mouths of tributary streams in rivers or at inlets where cold water enters lakes.

Since walleyes are usually found in groups, so are the fishermen who go after them. It's

Distribution: From Hudson Bay and Alberta south and east to western North Carolina, Alabama, and Tennessee.

Local names: Pike, yellow pike, walleye pike, pike perch, pickerel, yellow pickerel, dore.

← *"Hey Dad, this walleye's so heavy I'll bet it's a new world's record"*

not uncommon to see 20 or more boats slowly traveling back and forth or around a sand bar, with all fishermen catching fish. Sometimes, these boats are grouped extremely close together when the walleyes are hitting only in one small area.

Casting for walleyes either from a boat or from the shore of a lake or stream is exciting sport. Again, either live bait or artificial lures can be used. Many fishermen prefer to cast rather than troll for walleye since they believe casting frightens the fish less.

A third group of walleye fishermen favor still fishing to trolling or casting. Once they locate walleyes off a reef or bar, or in deeper water during warm weather, these fishermen anchor their boats and stay put. Live bait is used, sometimes with a spinner ahead of the bait. A light sinker keeps the bait on or near the bottom. Some anglers jig the rod up and down slowly giving "action" to the bait. Others place a sinker about two feet above the bait and slowly pump the rod up and down, bumping the sinker on the bottom each time the rod is lowered to make sure the bait is at the right depth.

Walleyes are predominantly nocturnal feeders but they are so voracious that they usually feed whenever food is available. Fishing for walleyes at night in shallow water close to shore is highly successful. Dusk is the time the walleye frequently moves into shore to feed on small fish which have also come into the shallows for food. The sound of walleyes feeding in the shallow water can often be heard on still nights. Anglers will often wade along the shallow water among the feeding walleyes. If great care is taken not to spook the fish either by noisy splashing, bumping rocks, or by flashing lights,

Fillets cooked for a shore lunch are part of the fun of walleye fishing

Walleyes are hitting!

Here's a sight familiar to any angler who uses a boat when fishing for walleyes. After a fisherman locates a school of walleyes, other boats soon congregate around him to get in on the fun.

Good walleye anglers locate where the first fish is caught by lining up several landmarks on shore to bisect the spot on the water. Then they either still fish or circle the spot at a slow speed, trolling for the walleyes until the school moves on to another feeding area.

an angler can work in close and catch these fish almost at his feet.

A walleye can sometimes be seen, or at least his tail is in evidence, while feeding in the shallows. Casting an artificial lure or live bait to one of these "tailing" fish will often bring an immediate strike. The lure or bait must be presented carefully, however, or the walleye may become frightened and leave the shallows.

Eyes of walleyes sensitive to light

These fish have the eyes specialized for low-light vision. They probably actively avoid lights. Hence, they may be found in shallow or deep water that is murky or turbid, but avoid shallows of clear water in the daylight. They may be caught in deep, clear water up to 60 feet in daytime.

Clean, cold water with sand bottom attracts this fish. They may live in muddy lakes but can't breed there so the stock must come from elsewhere.

Walleyes move to deeper water as the weather warms in the summer. Best fishing usually occurs in the spring and fall when the water is cold and the fish have not yet moved to the deep areas of the lake or stream. In some Southern areas, excellent walleye fishing occurs during the winter months.

Walleyes are primarily underwater fighters, rarely breaking the surface when hooked. Their tactics are dogged, without the dash or speed of a northern pike, but strong enough to provide great sport. This fish often dives under the net when the angler tries to land it.

Because of their tremendous appetites, they are almost constantly on the move looking for food. Tagged fish have been known to travel a 100 miles in less than a month, feeding in schools and moving as the food supply diminishes.

Spawning and walleye's early life

Spawning takes place in the spring in flowing waters of streams or along lake shores where wave action keeps the water moving. Usually a female is accompanied by more than one male and eggs are deposited over sand, gravel, or rocks. After spawning, the female returns immediately to deeper water but the males may linger in the spawning area for a short time. Neither fish guards the eggs or resulting fry.

The fry eat insects until they are two or three inches long, then change their diet to such small fish as yellow perch, suckers, minnows, or gizzard shad. Male walleyes reach sexual maturity at the end of the second year; females mature in their third year, averaging around 14 inches of length. The walleye competes for food with largemouth and smallmouth bass when all three fish are present in a lake or stream. The walleye spawns earlier and grows faster than either of the bass, hence more times than not, it wins the battle for available food. If enough walleyes are present in a body of water, populations of largemouth and smallmouth bass soon decline.

The walleye is excellent to eat and great numbers of these fish are sold fresh or frozen in fish markets. The meat is not oily and therefore will keep for long periods when frozen. The commercial netting of these fish is declining because of the tremendous surge of sport fishing and because of pressure from sports groups to save this fresh-water game fish for recreation rather than commercial use.

Sauger

Stizostedion canadense

The sauger has rows of dark spots along the spinous dorsal fin, plus large irregular dark body blotches that tend to fuse. The teeth are strong.

A great many fishermen catch saugers without realizing what kind of fish they have hooked, mistaking this fish for its relative, the walleye. There's no doubt that the sauger is similar to the walleye in body shape, but several distinct characteristics separate these two fishes. The sauger has large irregular dark body blotches and rows of black spots on the spinous dorsal whereas the walleye has a single black blotch toward the rear of the spinous dorsal and a white tip on the lower lobe of the tail.

The sauger lacks the popularity of the walleye, perhaps due to its limited range and average size. It generally runs smaller than the walleye, averaging about one pound, though large saugers weigh from 4 to 5 pounds. This fish reaches maturity in its third or fourth year; length seldom tops 15 inches. Some scientists suspect that 7- or 8-pound fish reputed to be saugers are hybrids between sauger and walleye.

The sauger shows a preference for large rivers, moving into lakes and tributary streams during breeding season. It can live in dirtier water than the walleye prefers, consequently does well in some of the more silty rivers. In the western part of its range, the sauger often lives in clear streams with sand bottom, feeding along shoals and sand bars at night.

Although in some areas the sauger is highly regarded by fishermen, most saugers are caught by anglers fishing for other species. They can be taken by trolling, casting, or still fishing.

When trolling, the boat should move slowly, similar to the speed used for walleyes. Saugers will hit a variety of artificial lures and can also be taken with a live bait-spinner combination or live bait alone. Jigs are popular as the sauger fisherman likes to fish on or close to the bottom. Drop-sinkers, often tied on a separate line from the spinner and minnow combination, keep the minnow off the bottom while the sinker bounces along the sand and rocks. Bucktails, streamer flies, and small spinners retrieved in a short jerky motion are effective at night when saugers go into the shallows or mouths of tributary streams to feed on small fish.

Distribution: Saskatchewan, Manitoba, and Ontario, south to West Virginia, Tennessee, and Alabama, and west to Wyoming, and Montana.

Local names: Sand pike, river pike, jackfish, spotfin pike.

Casting for saugers is especially popular in some of the large rivers. Again, artificial lures and live bait are effective. Many fishermen believe the best method of catching saugers in rivers is to still fish for them with live bait, usually minnows. Small frogs and night crawlers are widely used in some areas.

In some large rivers, like the Mississippi, the areas just below large dams are fruitful spots for sauger fishing. Saugers congregate in this swift water, foraging for food washed downstream. When a school of saugers is hitting, concentrations of boats can be seen anchored in the swift current below these dams.

New waters formed by large dams on the upper Missouri River have resulted in excellent sauger fishing. The waters below Garrison Dam in North Dakota and below the Ft. Randall Dam in South Dakota are producing ever increasing numbers of large saugers.

Sauger spawning takes place in the spring and the cycle is similar to that of the walleye. The fry feed on insects the first year, then switch their diet to small fish. At the end of the first year they reach a length of $2\frac{1}{2}$ to $4\frac{1}{2}$ inches. The sauger is also similar to the walleye in his voracious appetite and will feed during both day and night. Many sauger fishermen believe the nighttime hours to be the best for fishing.

Sauger is a tasty meat. The flesh resembles that of the walleye which is considered to be one of the best fresh-water fish to eat. Walleyes are often preferred over saugers because their average weight runs higher.

Sauger fishing "hot spots" lie in swift water below large river dams where schools of these fish forage for food.

Yellow perch

Perca flavescens

The he yellow perch is one of North America's most important sport fish. Its wide distribution, abundance, and willingness to take bait make it sport for a great number of anglers.

Yellow perch usually run in schools in both deep and shallow water of lakes, ponds, rivers, and reservoirs. When an experienced fisherman catches one, he tries the same spot again for others. During the spring and fall they can be taken near shore, around weed beds, docks, submerged rock piles, sunken logs and stumps. In the summer, as the water warms, yellow perch move into deeper, cooler water and are more difficult to catch.

This fish feeds almost entirely from the bottom so bait must be kept deep for best results. Flies, spinners, and spinner-fly combinations are effective artificial lures if retrieved slowly near the bottom of the lake or stream. But probably a majority of yellow perch are caught by fishermen using live bait, either worms or minnows. If the angler runs out of live bait, chunks of meat from a perch will usually fill the bill. Fly rods, spinning or casting tackle, or cane poles

The yellow perch has seven dark vertical bars on each side of the body. It has small teeth on jaws. The lower fins are deep yellow or orange in color.

make suitable tackle to catch this little fish.

Yellow perch spawn in early spring, as soon as the ice goes out in northern lakes and streams. Large schools may spawn in the shallow water of small bays. These fish do not build nests, but the female apparently purposely attaches her strings of eggs to underwater vegetation or rocks. The male fertilizes the eggs as they are released. The fry reach 2 to 4 inches by the end of the first season.

Yellow perch multiply rapidly and can easily overpopulate a lake, pond, or stream. When this happens, the fish are thin and stunted. For perch to attain a normal size, their numbers must be controlled by fishermen or by predators, or both. The yellow perch is a valuable food fish for walleye, northern pike, muskellunge, and lake trout.

In some waters, yellow perch become infested with parasitic worms which form cysts in the flesh. Although these cysts are unsightly, they do not prevent the use of the perch for food. The parasites are not harmful to humans and are killed in cooking.

Distribution: North-central Canada, Great Lakes area, east to Atlantic coast, south to Carolinas. North-central United States.

Local names: Perch, ringed perch, lake perch.

Ice fishing for perch

In many areas, fishing through the ice for yellow perch produces most of the annual catch. Since perch run in schools, fishermen often have to cut several holes in the ice to locate the fish.

Both artificial lures and live bait can be used when fishing through the ice. Short, stiff rods are best for this type of fishing since the fish must be lifted straight up when hooked.

Perch are hitting!

It's not unusual to see boats concentrated close together on a lake when a school of perch has been located.

Perch are easily located in the evening when they move in to shallow water near the shore to feed. Still fishing with bobbers or trolling the bait very slowly near the bottom are both good methods of catching yellow perch. Flies attract perch but they must be fished below the surface of the water. Yellow perch rarely take any food, natural or artificial, when it is presented on the surface.

To the dedicated walleye or pike fisherman, the yellow perch is sometimes a nuisance, taking the angler's minnow as fast as he rebaits the hook.

Codfish, drum and eel families

In areas where fishing opportunities are limited, freshwater drum, burbot, and American eel are pursued by local fishermen as vigorously as trout anglers after rainbows in Montana. In other parts of their range where traditional sporting fish are abundant, these fish are sometimes caught by anglers after other species.

Freshwater drum make an unusual drumming sound in and out of the water, the origin of which has long puzzled fishermen. Though sport fishing pressure for this fish is not great, he is an important commercial species in the Mississippi River.

The eel is caught by a great number of fishermen using a variety of methods including hook and line. Certainly not the most handsome of fish, the eel is nevertheless considered good to eat. Many tons are consumed each year in America and Europe.

Burbot feed on almost any kind of fish they can catch, which makes them candidates for a hook and line. In some areas, they provide sport when they can be caught through the ice.

Drum make a prize catch for this angler

← Just drum, who cares? It probably makes little difference to this youngster that some fishermen regard her catch of freshwater drum with something less than enthusiasm. She has caught a fine string of fish and is proud of it.

Burbot

Lota lota

The burbot is the only member of the codfish family to spend an entire lifetime in fresh water. It is regarded both as a sport fish and as a trash fish, depending upon what area of this country or Canada you happen to be in.

The burbot satisfies its voracious appetite by feeding primarily on other fish, including its own kind. This trait makes it fairly easy to catch in waters where it is abundant. Fishermen get best results with live bait; almost any kind will do. Many burbot are also caught on spinners and spoons. Anglers will find this fish in the deeper areas of cold water lakes and in some streams. Burbot grow to about three feet in length and may weigh from 10 to 16 pounds at maturity; most fish run smaller.

Areas in which the burbot is considered a nuisance have no conservation laws regarding limits or seasons on him. In some regions, however, the taking of burbot is restricted by law. Wyoming, for instance, considers the burbot a sport fish and regulations for hook and line fishermen are enforced.

Fishing through the ice for burbot has become a popular winter sport in some parts of the country. Live minnows are probably the favor-

Burbot has pectoral and pelvic fins, a single barbel below chin. Dorsal and anal fins are separate from tail. Tail is rounded.

ite bait for this type of fishing. In some states ice fishing is allowed through the January and March spawning season; during this period anglers search for it in shallow water. Tackle used for catching burbot through the ice need not be fancy. Many fishermen simply use a stick with a piece of heavy cord attached. This fish does not appear to be fussy about its food or how bait is presented.

The burbot is most active after dark; therefore, night fishing is more productive. Some anglers feel it bites best on dark nights and that it is usually more active in stormy and windy weather than when the night is clear and calm.

Conflict of opinions regarding burbot

This fish is destructive since it consumes large quantities of whatever smaller fish it can catch. In some areas, however, its value as a game fish overshadows its destructive habits.

Just as there is disagreement over the sporting qualities of this fresh-water member of the cod family, so is there disagreement over whether or not it is good to eat. Some fishermen regard the meat of the burbot as "strong flavored," others claim the flavor to be excellent. The large livers are sometimes used in making oil for commercial operations and for medicinal extracts.

Distribution: Found in Canada, Alaska, and the northern part of United States.

Local names: Fresh water cod, cusk, ling, eel-pout, and lawyer.

Freshwater drum

Aplodinotus grunniens

The freshwater drum, like the burbot, is the only member of its family to spend its entire life in fresh water. Members of the drum family are named for their ability to make a "drumming" sound in or out of the water. How they make this sound is debatable. Some scientists theorize that it is caused by the grinding of large throat teeth; others feel it may be the result of expelling air from one part of the air bladder to another.

Where valued fish abound, the drum is not considered a sport fish. Yet, in some areas can be found dedicated drum fishermen, enthusiastic about his sporting qualities.

The freshwater drum feeds the bottom of lakes, rivers, and streams. It often inhabits silty, still water but is also available in clean rivers and lakes. The average size for this drum runs from 1 to 2 pounds; 10 to 20 pounders are

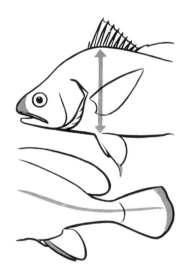

The snout is blunt, rounded, and overhung. Body widest at first dorsal. Pelvic fins have hairlike filaments. Ear bones or otoliths were treasured by Indians as good luck charms.

Lateral line extends into tail. Tail is rounded, the second spine in the anal fin is long and heavy.

sometimes caught, however. This is an important commercial fish in the Mississippi River.

Most fishermen use live bait for drum fishing, although occasionally it hits artificial lures presented by anglers casting or trolling for other species. Favorite baits include shrimp, worms, crayfish, or pieces of fish. Experienced anglers use a lightly weighted line to keep the hook on or near the bottom of the lake or stream; some keep the bait moving slowly. Many fishermen use more than one hook per line to increase their chances of enticing the drum to bite.

The freshwater drum, like the burbot, is considered good to eat by some sportsmen, while others completely reject it as table fare.

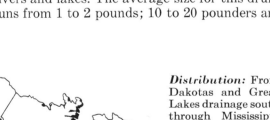

Distribution: From Dakotas and Great Lakes drainage south through Mississippi River to the Gulf of Mexico.

Local names: Gray bass, sheepshead, white perch, grunt, grunter, croaker, grinder, silver bass, gou, and gaspergou.

American eel

Anguilla rostrata

Many fishermen, somewhat repulsed by the eel's snakelike body, find it difficult to consider him a sport fish. Nonetheless, in spite of its unattractive appearance, the American eel is a true fish that plays an important role in both commercial and sport fishing. Many tons of eel reach American tables annually.

The eel's unusual life cycle limits information regarding its habits. Enough is known, however, to make its history one of the most interesting of any sport fish in North America.

Life cycle of the American eel

Ichthyologists long knew that in the spring young eels, called elvers, swim up fresh-water rivers and streams draining to the sea. They also knew that adult eels migrate downstream to the sea each fall. But once the adult eels reached salt water, scientists lost track of them. Where they spawned remained a mystery until a few years ago when a Danish scientist discovered the spawning grounds in the Sargasso Sea off Bermuda. All eels found in North America originate in this area set apart by floating seaweed.

The American eel has a mouth with jaws, a pectoral fin, a single pair of gill openings in front of pectoral fin; continuous fin from dorsal to anal regions.

A female eel carries as many as 15 million eggs and spawns down to a depth of fifteen hundred feet in water warmer and saltier than usual ocean water. After spawning, both male and female die.

The American eel requires about a year to go through the larval stage, hatching in spring and drifting northward with the Gulf Stream and arriving on the east coast of the United States the following winter. At this period it is a flat, transparent creature, called a leptocephalus. This name occurred when a German scientist gave the tiny larva a Latin name meaning "thinhead," not realizing it was actually a small eel. In the spring, the leptocephali change into rounded elvers about 2 to 4 inches long, closely resembling adults.

The female eel moves into fresh water

Once the elvers reach rivers and streams the males remain primarily in the brackish water, seldom moving more than a short distance into fresh water. The females are powerful swimmers and migrate upstream, many for amazingly long distances. Females occasionally travel thousands of miles inland. They climb waterfalls and low dams, slither over rocks and grass, and move through underground water passages. With this ability, it is easy to explain how eels

Distribution: Southern Greenland south along Eastern Canada and United States to Gulf Coast. Mississippi Valley inland to New Mexico, Kansas, Nebraska, South Dakota, Minnesota, and Wisconsin.

Local names: None

get into landlocked lakes. They have been known to squirm short distances overland in marshy or damp areas searching for food.

People along the Western States and coast of the United States and Canada often claim to find eels. These specimens always prove to be species of lampreys. So far an American eel has never been found west of the Continental Divide in North America.

Adult eels return to place of birth

The female eel spends anywhere from 5 to 20 years in lakes, ponds, or streams before migrating back to the sea to spawn. In this period she grows larger than the male, sometimes reaching a length of four feet or even more. Males rarely exceed 18 inches in length.

Once the female eel returns to salt water, her body changes to an almost silver color. Her digestive tract degenerates so that she cannot feed on her long, difficult trek back to the Sargasso Sea. At the coast the females are joined by the males for the trip to their spawning grounds. The males go through the same physical and coloration changes as the females.

The trip to the Sargasso Sea may take one or two months. Once under way the eels disappear. It is believed that the female's eggs mature during the journey to the spawning grounds, but a female full of mature eggs has yet to be caught by scientists.

In certain parts of eastern United States great numbers of eels are taken by hook and line anglers, either deliberately or while fishing for other species. Eels are often cut up to serve as bait for other sport fish. Most fishermen use worms or minnows for catching eels. The true eel angler will fish at night when the eel does most

of its feeding, but eels can be taken anytime.

Eels feed on small fish, crabs, shrimps, and worms. They will eat almost any animal food, living or dead, which makes them one of nature's scavengers. They prefer dead fish and have been known to completely devour fish in gill nets.

In extremely cold areas the eel buries herself in the mud during the winter months. In some states she can be taken by probing repeatedly the mud of lake and river bottoms with a multiple-pronged spear.

Eels can also be caught without using a hook on a line. Some anglers simply thread worms onto a piece of string lengthwise with a needle. After a number of worms are on the string, they wad up the end holding the worms and toss it into the water. The eel will grab the bait, get its teeth tangled in the string. Sometimes it is just too greedy to let go of the food. If the fisherman hauls in the string fast enough, the eel can be landed before it has a chance to untangle itself or let go of the bait.

Cleaning and cooking eel is simple

Skinning is the usual method for cleaning eel. Nail it through the head onto a board for stability, then cut the skin around its body just behind the head. With a pair of pliers, peel the skin, starting at the head and pulling toward the tail. Fresh eels are easiest to skin.

Eels are favored on tables both in Europe and the United States. In Europe eels are so popular as food that engineers design special tunnels around the dams to help elvers move up tributary streams to mature. The meat can be stewed, pickled, jellied, or broiled. Smoked eel is superb. New Englanders generally boil this fish, then flour and fry in butter.

Sunfish family

Luckily for North American anglers, the sunfish family is native only to this continent. These fish have won popularity with fishermen throughout the United States and Canada for their spunk on the line and their excellent flavor on the dinner table. It's difficult to surpass them for pure fishing enjoyment.

The 30 species of this family include the smallmouth and largemouth basses, claimed by many fishermen to be the scrappiest fighters for their weight of any species found in fresh water. The family also numbers such sunfish as rock bass, Sacramento perch, crappies, bluegills, warmouth, and pumpkinseed.

This prolific family requires frequent harvesting or they soon overpopulate a body of water. It's difficult to "fish out" water inhabited by these fish since they normally reproduce faster than they are caught.

In addition to being plentiful, the sunfish family is easy to catch with a variety of tackle and methods. Dry flies, surface and underwater lures, small live minnows, worms, crayfish, spinners, and spoons—all are effective. The idea is to get a bait or lure in the water—some member of this family will usually take care of the rest.

There's no finer fighter than a largemouth

← Whether you fish with live bait or spinners, wobbling spoons or surface poppers, the largemouth hits like a freight train and fights both on the surface and below. He's fast and stubborn, and more times than not will fling your lure high in the air just when you think you have him whipped.

Largemouth bass

Micropterus salmoides

Largemouth bass has upper jaw extending behind the eye. Fish is usually dark green on the back, lighter green on sides, greenish to white on belly.

Deep notch between dorsal fins; usually 13 soft rays. Dark stripe extends full length of body.

Distribution: In southern Canada, throughout the United States and in northern Mexico.

Local names: Largemouth, slough bass, Oswego bass, black bass, green trout.

Weed bed fishing for largemouth bass

This angler is fishing small open areas between stumps →
and weed beds where the bass often search for food.
Some fishermen cast deliberately onto pads, retrieve
slowly allowing the lure to slip into the open spaces.

The largemouth bass is one of the most popular sport fish in North America. Not only does its range cover a good share of the United States and southern Canada, but it's available at almost all seasons and will hit a variety of baits and artificial lures. When hooked, it's a spunky fighter that demands respect; permitted slack line, it stands on tail, easily throws a lure.

The largemouth prefers warm and sluggish waters of sloughs and bayous; it thrives in weedy, mud-bottomed lakes, ponds, and streams. For this reason it's a favorite stocking fish in reservoirs and farm ponds. An adult largemouth is not finicky about its diet but feeds on many species of small fishes (including its own fry), frogs, crayfishes, worms, tadpoles, and insects.

Artificial surface lures used with spinning or bait-casting tackle are popular equipment for catching this fish. The largemouth bass will of-ten leap clear of the water and take a plug on the way down. Deep or moderately deep-running lures will also attract this bass, especially on hot summer days when it is in deeper waters. Popper bugs and flies with a fly rod is the time-honored method for taking bass. A medium-size largemouth on a light fly rod will give any angler a tough battle.

Bait fishing for largemouths is popular in some parts of the country. Largemouths feed on many species of small fish making them candidates for a live minnow, or other bait fish, used by itself or in combination with a spinner. Worms account for hooking a great many large-mouths, as do frogs fished on the surface and crayfish fished deep. Weighted plastic worms and eels are particularly good in the South, with black being the favorite color.

Fish for this bass near weed beds, sunken logs, brush piles, or in the waters of quiet

bays and sloughs. It is usually found in fairly shallow water; weedy shore lines are ideal for largemouth bass fishing. It can be caught any time of the day or night but early morning and early evening are usually best.

Largemouth bass vary considerably in size, depending upon the area in which they are found. The largest fish inhabit warm waters of the south where a food supply is plentiful and waters remain at a temperature conducive to feeding the year around. Specimens weighing 10 pounds or more are often caught in this area,

Surface lure results in a good catch

Spinning tackle and surface lures are ideal for the young fisherman angling for largemouth bass. These fish were caught on a popping lure cast to the edge of a weed bed, then retrieved slowly by jerking rod.

Florida Everglades produce good catches of largemouth bass year around

Numerous farm ponds stocked with largemouth bass offer excellent fishing and help increase fish's popularity.

with Florida consistently producing large fish.

This bass spawns in late winter in the south and begins to spawn in May in northern waters depending upon the water temperature. Spawning usually takes place in shallow, quiet waters or bays or sloughs where the male largemouth excavates a nest two feet wide and 4 or more inches deep by tail fanning, then drives a female into the nest to deposit her eggs. He guards the eggs and later the fry after hatching. Largemouth bass do not nest in communal areas as do many of the smaller sunfish.

Largemouths thrive in alkaline lakes

This Montana lake is typical of many barren western areas where the largemouth has helped revive fishing in reservoirs and lakes unsuited for other species.

Smallmouth bass

Micropterus dolomieui

Distribution: Originally only in Great Lakes, St. Lawrence River system, and upper Mississippi, Ohio, and Tennessee Rivers. Introduced in all areas of North America.

Local names: Smallmouth, smallmouth black bass, redeye bass, bronzeback.

Upper jaw extends to middle of eye. Cheek scales smaller than on largemouth. Lines radiate from the snout and eye.

Shallow notch between dorsal fins; usually 14 soft dorsal rays. Vertical stripes or blotches on body.

Smallmouth water

This successful smallmouth bass fisherman knows that the secret to good catches lies in finding a spot with rocks, or a sand and gravel bottom. Casting to the point where a rock cliff meets the water is often productive. With a surface lure, anglers let the plug lie quietly for a moment after the cast, then twitch the line a few times before beginning the retrieve. Smallmouths will often hit a lure fished this way when they won't take a lure that is retrieved immediately.

In the spring and late fall the fisherman often switches to the fly rod with streamers and wet flies. Smallmouths are a type of fish where many lures and methods should be tried at different depths until a productive combination is found.

Fishermen have long debated the relative fighting merits of the smallmouth bass against those of the other species of fresh-water fish. Whether the smallmouth can claim the champion's title has to be decided by the individual angler, but few deny that when hooked it is a great fighter for its weight.

Where its largemouth cousin prefers warm, sluggish water, the smallmouth inhabits the cooler clear lakes and rivers. Gravel or rock bottom lakes with strong currents and rapids, or riffles connecting two lakes are especially good spots for this fish.

Adult smallmouths are rarely found in small streams, though juvenile bass occasionally move into these waters. In large, fast-moving rivers, this bass inhabits areas liberally sprinkled with sand, gravel, and rock, but avoids weed beds or other submerged vegetation favored by the largemouth bass.

The life habits of the smallmouth bass during the cold winter months remain somewhat of a mystery. It is believed to reduce its food consumption and to retreat to deep water as the colder temperatures reach the lakes and rivers. When the water temperature drops to about 50 degrees, the smallmouth bass becomes inactive and catching this fish at that time is nearly impossible. A few are taken through the ice in early fall and early spring, but catches of this member of the sunfish family are limited.

The smallmouth bass feeds on small fish plus crayfish, grasshoppers, dragonflies, May flies, beetles, and many types of small flies. Because of its wide range of diet, it can be caught on almost all types of fishing tackle, both by trolling and casting methods. This versatility probably accounts for the smallmouths' popularity with so many anglers.

On a fly rod, this fish provides enough action to keep the most expert fisherman quite busy. It will hit both wet and dry flies. A variety of surface lures are also effective for taking the smallmouth. Its attack of a surface plug often consists of spectacular leaps and splashes that seem to indicate a much larger fish. Spinning tackle is growing in popularity with smallmouth fishermen who prefer to cast small artificial lures and baits a long distance, an advantage in this type of fishing.

Many anglers favor working rocky points and rock shelves along the shore of lakes and rivers from early sunset to dark. Their boat is kept within casting distance of shore so lures land within inches of the rocks where these fish lie in wait. If smallmouths are not hitting surface lures anglers switch to bucktails or marabou jigs and go deep after them.

Bait-casting equipment combined with any one of many underwater lures is effectively used by fishermen in pursuit of the smallmouth bass. Large numbers of these fighting fish are also

Fish the fast water

The smallmouth bass prefers water with some motion, so these two fishermen are trying their luck in the fast water below a spillway. Construction of dams and spillways on many large rivers has provided suitable water for smallmouth bass. However, in many areas, dams and spillways have resulted in decreased smallmouth fishing because of the lowering of the water level.

Clear, moving rivers are prime waters for the smallmouth fisherman, as the deep holes, rocks, boulders, and gravel afford the bronzeback ample habitat for its active type of living. And with the current to help in its battle with the fisherman, it is a match for the best of equipment and angler's skill.

caught by live bait fishermen, with a minnow and spinner combination the favorite bait. Regardless of the fishing lure or method used, the smallmouth bass can be expected to put up a strong battle on and below the surface of the water.

The smallmouth bass spawns in the spring in water 6 feet deep or less. The area chosen usually has a gravel, sand, or rock bottom clear of vegetation. A favorite spawning location is near a large submerged rock or stump. The male smallmouth builds the nest by tail fanning, then fertilizes the eggs deposited by the female. The eggs cling to the pebbles or rock; the male protects the nest and the newborn young. After the young are hatched the male fish will herd the tiny, black fry near shore and keep them there by diligently patrolling the area. The small fish remain under guard for about 10 days until they are old enough to go their separate ways.

Some of the best smallmouth waters are the Thousand Islands area of the St. Lawrence River, Lake Nippissing and other lakes of southern Ontario, particularly Lake of the Woods, and the Bass Islands of Lake Erie. The Ozark Mountain area in Missouri and Arkansas is also famous for smallmouth bass fishing. Since these fish prefer cool water, they do not occur in waters of the far south.

Smallmouth bass are excellent to eat; they clean easily by filleting, and the flesh is firm and delicious.

Float fishing for smallmouth bass

These anglers are floating down a river fishing the deeper holes where smallmouths prefer to live. That spot under the rock overhang looks particularly good.

Spinning gear pays off

Light spinning tackle and small lures increase the excitement of smallmouth fishing. This fisherman cast near a pile of submerged rocks for his catch. Some anglers prefer to release their fish at water level.

Fishing at sunset

Smallmouths often move into → shallow water to feed at late evening. On a quiet night such as this when insects hatch is a perfect time for fishing from the lake shore or river bank.

Spotted bass

Micropterus punctulatus

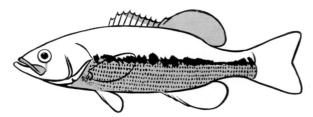

Similar to smallmouth in head and dorsal fins. Lateral band appears less regular than largemouth; black dots in rows, below lateral band, form stripes. Tongue has teeth. Soft dorsal rays usually number 12.

The spotted bass, although closely related to the smallmouth, is a distinct species of the sunfish family. Its physical appearance is a cross between the largemouth and smallmouth, though it is smaller than either of these fish. Maximum size for spotted bass runs about 18 inches in length and 4 pounds in weight. It is an excellent sporting fish; when taken on a light line this spunky fighter puts any angler to the test. In the southern part of its range, this bass is available year around.

Either artificial lures or live bait attract the spotted bass. Spoons, plugs, and spinners are especially effective. Many live bait fishermen use minnows for bait with worms being a close second choice.

The spotted bass prefers pool and riffle streams with a firm bottom, usually sand or gravel. It can often be found in the cool, clear headwaters of such streams. In some parts of its range it moves into deep parts of lakes. For instance in some southern reservoirs the spotted bass inhabits depths of over 100 feet, while smallmouths will be above 60 feet, and largemouths up to or near the surface.

During the fall, the spotted bass inhabiting rivers migrate downstream to winter in deep water pools; in the spring they move back upstream for the summer. At spawning time the male fish takes on the domestic chores of building the nest, fertilizing and guarding the eggs after they are deposited by the female and later protecting the fry until they are old enough to fend for themselves. The young spotted bass feed on insects and insect larvae until they are grown, then switch their diet to small fish, frogs, and crayfish.

Experienced northern anglers must change their fishing techniques slightly to catch this southern fish. The spotted bass, like the smallmouth and largemouth found in the south, will lie in tight quarters beneath under-cut banks or beneath water hyacinths. The angler's plug or fly must hit close by or the fish will never see it. Fishermen often cast several times into a good hole before enticing the bass out with a perfect cast. Weedless lures take much of the strain out of fishing some areas.

Distribution: Ohio and Virginia southwest to gulf. East to western Florida.

Local names: Kentucky bass, Kentucky spotted bass.

Redeye bass

Micropterus coosae

Because the range of the redeye bass covers a relatively small area, many fishermen are unfamiliar with this fish. Veteran anglers who have fished for him, however, claim the redeye is an excellent sport fish with an aggressive fighting spirit. One of the largest redeye bass on record weighed just a little over 4 pounds, but the average weight of fish taken by fishermen runs a pound or less.

The redeye bass usually inhabits small streams at the higher elevations of its distribution area, preferring cooler and clearer waters than most warm-water fish. A number of rivers within its range produce good catches of redeyes. Sheeds Creek and Spring Creek, Tennessee, offer excellent redeye bass fishing. One of the largest redeye bass caught by a fisherman came from the Chattahoochee River in Alabama.

This colorful little fish migrates downstream about the time the first heavy frost occurs, to spend the winter in pools of rivers at lower elevations. In the spring, it swims back upstream and is usually in its summer habitat by April.

The redeye bass has many of the characteristics of the brook trout. It is similar in size, habitat preference, feeding habits, and fighting ability. However, the redeye is definitely a bass and is closely related to the spotted bass.

This bass is primarily a surface feeder on insects and insect larvae. The redeye also feeds to a limited extent on small fish. Surface feeding makes it possible to catch him with artificial surface lures as well as live bait. Catching a fish that feeds on the surface provides a dramatic, explosive battle. Whatever the lure, the smash

The redeye bass has mouth and dorsal fin shape similar to smallmouth. No dark middle stripe present. Adults often have red eyes, reddish fins. Dorsal fin usually has 12 soft rays.

of a redeye is a startling thrill to any fisherman. A fly rod with a light lure or fly, or spinning tackle and lures are good combinations for taking redeyes.

Many fishery experts believe the redeye bass can become a more important game fish than it is at present. This bass is a fairly new addition to the list of North American game fishes so its full potential has not been explored. Since the redeye does well in waters too warm for trout but too small for most game fish, scientists believe that it has potentialities in waters which at present lack good sport fish.

Distribution: Southeastern streams from Alabama to Savannah Rivers. Western Florida.

Local names: Shoal bass.

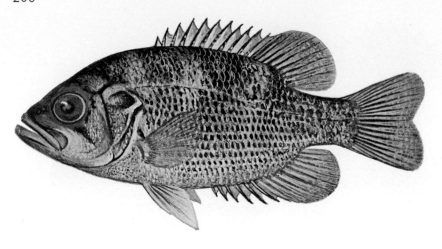

Rock bass are identified by their red eye and large mouth.

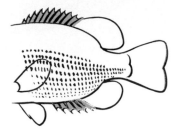

Base of each scale dark, forming rows of dots; 5-7 anal spines, 11 dorsal spines.

Rock bass

Ambloplites rupestris

Many rock bass are caught by anglers fishing for smallmouth bass. These two fish inhabit the same waters in many areas. The rock bass is a scrapper like the smallmouth, although smaller in size.

The largest specimens of rock bass rarely exceed 12 inches in length and seldom weigh more than a pound. Most fish caught by anglers run much smaller, from 4 to 7 inches in length.

Rock bass can be found in lakes, streams, or ponds. This fish prefers drop-offs, rocky points, and shallow gravelly areas for its habitat. Sunken trees and logs are especially fruitful places to catch rock bass and can be reached by using a weedless lure.

The rock bass seems to be a gregarious fish, preferring to travel in schools. When an angler takes one fish, chances are good more can be coaxed from the same area. Live bait is the most effective method of fishing for this sunfish, with worms the first choice of many fishermen. The rock bass will also take wet or dry flies. A small spinner attached ahead of the fly often brings desired results.

This little fellow hits a bait or fly aggressively with the force of a much larger fish. Once hooked, it usually fights vigorously, swimming in a tight circle attempting to throw the hook. Rock bass are often caught on a variety of artificial and natural baits while trolling or casting for walleyes and northern pike. Their first strike is strong enough to fool any angler into thinking he has a solid hit of a walleye or northern and the inexperienced fisherman is often surprised when he hauls in this aggressive, chunky battler.

The largest rock bass are usually found in lakes. Those caught in smaller streams may be stunted due to inadequate food supply. This fish feeds primarily on insects although he will eat small fish and crayfish.

Spawning takes place in the spring and the method is similar to that of other sunfishes. The male builds the nest on gravelly bottom by fanning his tail over the nest area. After the eggs are deposited by the female, they are guarded by the male; he also stays with the fry for a short while.

Because they easily adapt to a variety of water conditions, rock bass have been introduced into many new areas. They are good to eat, especially when taken from clear, cold water. Unfortunately many of these fish are covered with parasites in some northern lakes, making them unsightly and shunned by the sportsmen catching meat for the dinner table.

Distribution: Saint Lawrence River and Great Lakes, except Lake Superior, southern Canada, through Mississippi drainage to Gulf Coast.

Local names: Goggle-eye, redeye, rock sunfish.

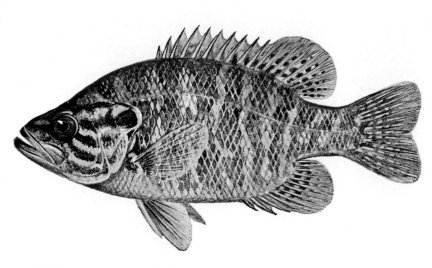

Large mouth, dark stripes radiating from eye and snout.

Spots form rows on soft dorsal. Irregular bars on body; 3 anal spines. Tongue has teeth.

Warmouth

Chaenobryttus gulosus

In spite of being one of the larger panfish of the sunfish family, the warmouth is a shy fish. It prefers lakes or ponds with mud bottoms and containing a great many weeds, stumps, and other hiding places. This sunfish at maturity may reach a pound in weight and about a foot in length. Average size of warmouth caught by most anglers, however, is much smaller, but still a scrapper.

Warmouths will take artificial flies and are great sport on a fly rod. Most fly-rod fishing for warmouths is done early in the season before the weed growth in lakes and ponds makes landing the fish difficult. This fish will also take small surface lures; many are caught on small fly-rod poppers.

Late in the season, the best method of catching warmouths is to use a cane pole to drop the bait into the openings in the weeds and haul the fish out before it becomes tangled in the vegetation. Worms can be used as bait, and minnows are good. The warmouth is carnivorous to a greater degree than most sunfish, and the main item of food in its diet is small fish. It also feeds on snails and crustaceans.

The warmouth prefers to build its spawning nest in silty mud or in mud containing weeds, sticks, and leaves. It particularly seeks out the quiet backwater lakes of larger rivers. Where possible, it will build its nest close to stumps, roots, and rocks. Unlike other sunfish, the warmouth isn't especially particular about water depth for spawning, but may spawn close to shore or in the middle of the lake.

The male guards the nest during spawning. Unlike other sunfish, once the eggs hatch the young fish are not guarded by the male who allows them to scatter immediately into dense weeds or other hiding places. The fry, feeding upon insects, reach up to 2 inches in length the first year. As they grow larger they add small fish to their diet and by the end of the third year reach maturity.

In areas where the warmouth is abundant it is a very popular sport fish. It is an edible fish, especially when caught in clean water, but is not considered as desirable in flavor as the rock bass or bluegill. Any fish that inhabits areas of mud bottom, heavy vegetation, and feeds on animals that live in the mud, will be less palatable than those living above clean gravel or a rock bottom.

Warmouths are quite often confused with rock bass due to coloration, markings, and similarity of habits. Many fishermen forget the field identification which distinguishes these two fish. A simple method of identification is to pull the stiff spines forward on the anal fin and count the number of sharp points—6 on the rock bass, only 3 on the warmouth.

Distribution: Kansas, Mississippi River drainage, east to New York and south to Gulf Coast.

Local names: Goggle-eye, stumpknocker, mud bass.

Small mouth ahead of the eye.
Ear flap has black margin.

Black spot or blotch on back
of soft part of dorsal fin. Pectoral fin long, pointed.

Bluegill

Lepomis macrochirus

Ounce for ounce, the bluegill is undoubtedly one of the scrappiest sport fish. Fishermen value it not only because it's fun to catch but also because it makes up an important source of food for other sport fish. This little sunfish is abundant in most areas of the United States. Although not native to all parts of the country, it has been widely stocked in both artificial and natural lakes.

Bluegills do not grow large. Under ideal conditions the average size will run about 12 inches in length, but if the waters are overstocked, it may grow no larger than about 3 inches. Overstocking is a definite problem with bluegills. They multiply very fast and if not eaten by other fish or caught by fishermen, their numbers soon exceed the available food supply.

Usually bluegills inhabit moderately shallow water. Fish for them near weed beds, in quiet bays or inlets, and around stumps and submerged logs. They can be caught with a variety of tackle and bait. Children, and adults too, with cane poles and a few worms have a good time catching this fish. Fly-rod fishing for bluegills is wonderful sport, or just still fishing with a casting rod is fun.

On a fly rod, the bluegill is a worthy opponent. It hits the lure hard and its fight, when hooked, usually takes it in fast circles. Its flat body provides a good deal of leverage at the end of a line. They will hit dry flies, wet flies, or small artificial lures such as poppers and small spinners. Worms are probably the most common live bait used.

Spawning takes place in late spring or early summer. The male fish moves into shallow water and builds a nest 6 inches to 2 feet in diameter. A rim of sand or silt, created by the fanning action of its fins, encircles the nest. As many as 50 of these nests can often be found in a relatively small area. When the nest is complete, the female deposits the eggs and the male guards them and resulting fry. The male hovers stationary over the nest ready to charge the enemy.

Distribution: Southern Ontario and Quebec south across the United States to Gulf. Introduced in many areas.

Local names: Brim, bream, copperhead, blue sunfish, sun perch, pumpkinseed.

Poppin' for bluegills is great sport

The popper lure and fly rod used by this angler is a →
favorite rig of many bluegill fishermen. Evenings and early morning when bluegills are feeding on insects in shallow water is the best time for lures.

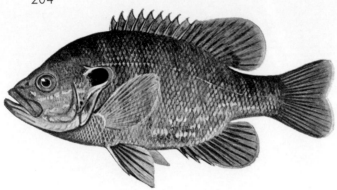

Green sunfish

Lepomis cyanellus

Large mouth extending almost to middle of eye, emerald dots on head. Ear flap black with light or pinkish border.

Light margin around edge of dorsal, tail and anal fins. Pectoral fin rounded. Tongue lacks teeth.

Pumpkinseed

Lepomis gibbosus

Small mouth, turquoise stripes and bands on head. Ear flap black with semicircular red spot on back edge.

Pumpkinseed has diffused spots on the dorsal fin. Pectoral fin is long and upper tip pointed.

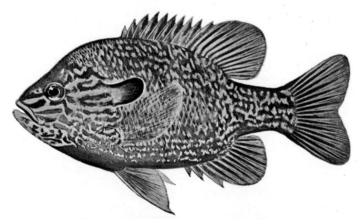

Longear sunfish

Lepomis megalotis

Mouth is moderately large, blue and reddish stripes on head. Ear flap black, long with red or light border along edge.

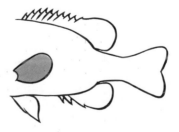

Longear males are reddish in color, mostly on breast and abdomen. Pectoral fin is short and rounded.

Distribution: From Colorado and South Dakota east to Minnesota, southern Ontario, New York. South through Great Lakes and Mississippi River System to Alabama.

Local names: Blue-spotted sunfish, rubbertail, green perch, sand bass, bream, sunfish.

The green sunfish is usually most abundant in small streams but is also found in various size lakes and ponds over a wide range. What it lacks in size it makes up for in scrappiness which makes it a fine fish for young fishermen.

Distribution: Minnesota and southern Canada east across the United States to the Atlantic, south to South Carolina. Pennsylvania, Ohio, west to Iowa.

Local names: Common sunfish, yellow sunfish, flatfish.

The pumpkinseed has been introduced on the west coast, in addition to other areas, both for sport and to serve as food for other species.

Distribution: From Minnesota and lower Great Lakes, south through Mississippi River drainage system. Also found in southwestern United States.

Local names: Big-eared sunfish, red-bellied bream, blackears, redbreast, red perch.

A close look for difficult extraction

Small mouths plus a greedy appetite spell trouble in removing hooks from panfish. It is best to use small hooks with long shanks to relieve this problem. Also, set hook quickly so the fish doesn't swallow the bait.

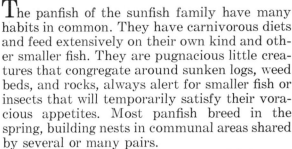The panfish of the sunfish family have many habits in common. They have carnivorous diets and feed extensively on their own kind and other smaller fish. They are pugnacious little creatures that congregate around sunken logs, weed beds, and rocks, always alert for smaller fish or insects that will temporarily satisfy their voracious appetites. Most panfish breed in the spring, building nests in communal areas shared by several or many pairs.

Among these panfish the green sunfish is most common due to his aggressiveness. It can be caught with a fly rod and small flies, tiny spinning lures, or probably most effectively, worms. This little fish is always a good battler when taken on light tackle.

Probably most green sunfish are caught by anglers fishing for the larger member of the sunfish family, the bluegill. It can be found in streams where the current is slow or in lakes or ponds where the bottom is muddy.

The pumpkinseed sunfish rarely exceeds 8 inches in length and averages much smaller. Because of its size it lacks popularity among fishermen. It can be caught using the same equipment and methods as those employed in bluegill fishing, especially over spawning beds.

This fish is considered a pest in many waters. It multiplies very rapidly if not controlled by heavy fishing or natural enemies.

The longear sunfish is often confused with the pumpkinseed and bluegill. In the north, it is generally smaller than either of these fish, rarely attaining 8 inches in length. This chunky little fish is found in both lakes and streams and has been introduced into many small ponds. It prefers clear water, but is occasionally found in somewhat murky, silty water.

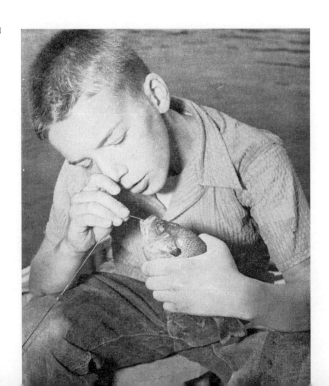

The redbreast, redear, and the spotted sunfishes are important sport fish, especially in the eastern and southeastern part of the United States. These fish are all spunky fighters and provide the angler with exciting fun when taken on a light tackle. They are also favorites of many youngsters because they hit bait readily and often.

The redbreast sunfish inhabits ponds, lakes, streams, or slow-moving rivers, but occasionally can be found in fast moving water. Its cousin the redear sunfish is primarily a fish of larger bodies of quiet water. The redear is an excellent stocking fish and is often used in combination with largemouth bass and bluegills for stocking farm ponds or small lakes. It hybridizes readily with the bluegill. The spotted sunfish lives primarily in small streams but is also present to some extent in large rivers.

All three of these sunfishes are similar to the bluegill in life habits. They will take bait, artificial lures, dry and wet flies. Though worms are the most popular bait, small spinning lures are often effective, especially for the redbreast and redear which average somewhat larger in size than the spotted sunfish. A variety of angling techniques can be used to catch panfish. By employing a light bobber, generally made from porcupine quills, the angler is able to see the gentle tug of sunfish. The quill lies flat on the surface and tilts up when the line is tightened.

Fly-rod fishing for sunfish with popper bugs makes top sport for people who may not have access to prime trout water. In some areas a light short leader with a wet fly is attached to the popper. In case they are not hitting surface lines the wet fly makes an attractive secondary bait. The popper aids in an easy retrieve.

Distribution: From Maine to Lake Ontario. South, east of Appalachian Mountains to Alabama and Florida. Introduced in other areas.

Local names: Red brim, robin, redbelly, bream.

Redbreast sunfish are the size of pumpkinseed. Many of these smaller species of the sunfish family make interesting aquarium fish. Check local game laws for possible conflict, however, before you carry some home.

Distribution: Original range in Georgia, Florida, Alabama, and lower Mississippi Valley. Has been introduced in Indiana, Ohio, Oklahoma, and other states.

Local names: Shellcracker, yellow bream, pond perch.

An unusual method of fishing for sunfish (bream) in the south is by sticking many cane poles out of a boat in all directions. This method, called shotgun or scatter gun fishing with multiple baits, is illegal in some northern states.

Distribution: From South Carolina to Florida. In the Mississippi Valley from Illinois to Texas.

Local names: Spotted bream, stumpknocker.

Small, yes, but they're keepers

Sunfish are ideal species for youngsters with little fishing experience. These fish are not usually shy and will take a variety of baits or lures regardless of fishing technique or lack of patience.

The redbreast sunfish has light blue streaks on head. Ear flap is black, long. Fish has moderate mouth.

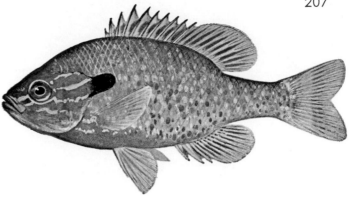

Pectoral fin is small. Spawning fish have orange-red breast.

Redbreast sunfish

Lepomis auritus

Redear sunfish has black ear flap with red or orange border. Head is without orange or blue wavy lines.

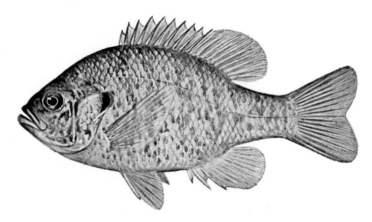

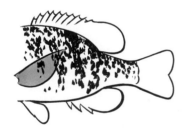

Body of fish has many dark or olive spots. Pectoral fin long, pointed.

Redear sunfish

Lepomis microlophus

Spotted sunfish has ear flap which is stiff and short. The head has no streaks or bars present.

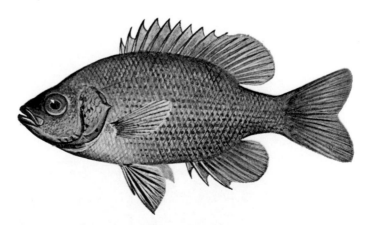

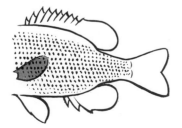

Fish has black or red spots on each scale which form even rows along body. Pectoral fin is small and quite rounded.

Spotted sunfish

Lepomis punctatus

Short dorsal fin with 6 spines. Base of dorsal, if projected, reaches just past the back of the head. Dark vertical bars on light colored body.

White crappie

Pomoxis annularis

Both the white and black crappies are excellent sport fish for anglers of all ages. These fish have similar life cycles and habitat preference. However, the white crappie withstands water that has more siltation than the black crappie, which has a preference for clear, weedy lakes or large streams and ponds.

The average-size crappie runs about 10 or 12 inches in length. These aggressive little fighters are taken with spinning lures, wet or dry flies, worms, minnows or crayfish. Small minnows are especially effective bait.

Though these fish are occasionally caught in deep water, best fishing spots are in or near weed beds. Where one crappie is caught, chances are that others will be near by.

Spawning habits are similar to those of the bluegill. A school of crappies will often build nests close together but usually spawn in deeper water than preferred by the bluegill.

Distribution: Nebraska east to Lake Ontario, and south through Ohio, Mississippi rivers.

Local names: White bass, silver crappie, papermouth.

Distribution: Southern Canada south through Great Lakes, Mississippi River System to Texas, northern Florida. Introduced in many other areas of United States.

Local names: Calico bass, speckled perch, tinmouth.

Black crappie

Pomoxis nigromaculatus

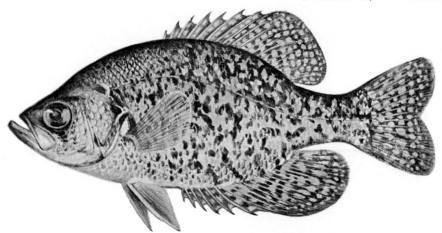

Long dorsal fin with 7 or 8 spines. Projected length of base of dorsal fin reaches to the eye. Body blotched with dark spots.

Fly-rod fishing accents the fun of catching this scrappy fighter

In some areas, the black or white crappie, or both provide the best fishing available to anglers. These fish can be taken throughout the year in some parts of their range and limits are often liberal. Crappies are similar to other sunfish in that overpopulation of a lake or stream may result in thin, stunted fish. In some waters, fishing through the ice for crappies has become a most popular winter sport.

Distribution: Virginia to Florida. Louisiana north in Mississippi River System to Indiana.

Local names: Round sunfish

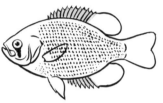

Spotted scales make even rows along the body. Dorsal fin spines number 11-13; anal fin spines 7 or 8.

Flier

Centrarchus macropterus

Equipment needn't be fancy for the angler to enjoy catching the flier. Cane pole, fly rod, willow stick, casting, or spinning tackle are all suitable. Like other members of the sunfish family, the flier satisfies its voracious appetite on insects, worms, and small fish. Small insects including mosquito larvae comprise its principal diet. In appearance, it's similar to a crappie.

The flier inhabits weedy sections of streams, bayous, or lakes. It will rise to a wet or dry fly but is usually taken with worms. This little battler rarely exceeds 6 inches in length and for that reason is not particularly favored among fishermen for its eating qualities.

Although the Sacramento perch was originally abundant in sloughs and slow-flowing channels of the Sacramento-San Joaquin River system, it is now isolated in a few California lakes and alkaline lakes of Western Nevada. Recently it has been stocked experimentally in sand hill lakes of the Plains states where alkaline content will not support other fresh-water fishes.

Principal diet of this sunfish includes small fish and water insects. Worms and live minnows are favored baits. It averages 7 to 9 inches in length; a 10 inch fish is considered large. The perch does not guard its eggs; other fish feed heavily on them, reducing the population.

Sacramento perch

Archoplites interruptus

Vertical bars and blotches. Dorsal fin has 12 or 13 spines; anal fin's spines number 6 or 7.

Distribution: Sacramento-San Joaquin drainage, Pajaro River System in California. Introduced in other areas.

Local names: None

Chapter **7**

How to clean fish

Scaling and skinning

Some methods of cleaning fish are based on speed, others adapt to the saving of every bit of meat. The main thing is to get the job completed while the fish is fresh; a day-or-two-old fish is miserable business to clean. Proper tools are important. In addition to pliers for holding the fish, and thin bladed knives and snippers for skinning, the angler will find many tools to aid in this project.

Dressing panfish

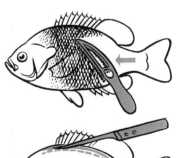

1 Smaller species are scaled and dressed in this manner. Scrape off scales toward the head with knife or scraper.

4 Continue cutting to pectoral fin. Lay fish flat and make deep cut on both sides of body behind pectoral fin.

2 Hold knife parallel to fins; cut along each side of dorsal and anal fins ¼ to ½ inch deep for later extraction.

5 Break backbone by pulling head upward. Head will tear loose; entrails, pectoral, and pelvic fins will be removed.

3 Hold inverted fish with its back resting on table and cut immediately behind vent. Slip knife forward under skin.

6 Remove dorsal and anal fins, loosened in Step 2, by pulling away and forward from the body. Cut off tail.

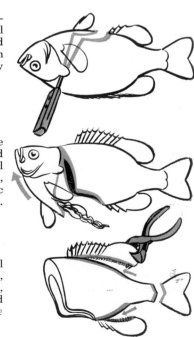

Cleaning trout

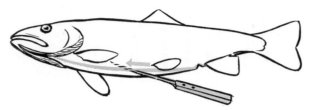

1 Clean trout as soon as possible after catching by inserting a knife at vent and slitting belly forward to gills. Some anglers cut a V-notch at the vent.

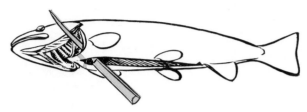

3 Place a finger in belly slit and gill opening and separate side of body from gills and gill rakers. Insert knife and cut loose at bottom on both sides.

2 Insert knife and cut at point where gill attachment, under the throat at base of branchiostegal rays, forms a V joining the lower belly to the head.

4 Stick finger in the gill throat and tear out gills and gill rakers. Entrails pull out with gills or remove next. Blood streak along spine should be removed.

Skinning bullheads

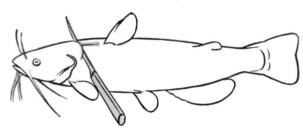

1 Bullheads should be fresh for easy skinning. Cut across top of back to backbone between head and dorsal fin. A short cut toward dorsal helps tear skin.

3 Push head downward, breaking backbone where knife made cut across back, removing entrails, belly flesh, and front fins along with head in one motion.

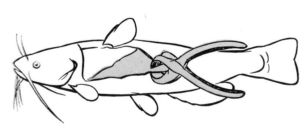

2 Pull skin toward tail with pliers; one pull on each half should tear off skin. Second side will pick up what skin is missed on tearing off the first side.

4 Other fins and tail may be removed before cooking, if desired. Large catfish need more slitting of skin around head, along back, and belly before skinning.

Filleting: *Walleyes, northern pike, bass*

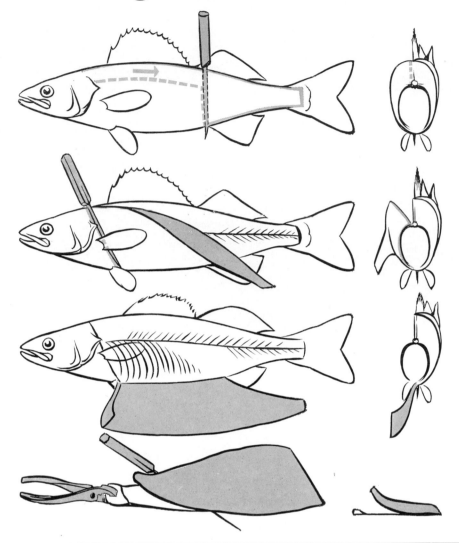

1 To fillet, saving the maximum of meat and minimum of bones try this method: Cut along back on one side of dorsal fin. Insert blade clear through body and out belly just behind vent. Slice along edge of anal fin, with blade sliding along backbone until reaching tail. Cut fillet loose and repeat on other side.

2 Slice diagonally from top of back to belly just behind head, pectoral fin, and pelvic fin. Repeat slice on other side of body, or finish one side at a time.

3 Insert knife blade in original cut (Step 1) and slice downward freeing meat from rib cage. After working down over main part of ribs, keep cutting as close against lower ribs as possible until reaching belly. Cut through belly, separating fillet from body.

4 Lay fillet skin down on table. With heavy, flat knife cut down into fillet leaving tab for holding skin. Pull on skin and use knife in a seesaw motion. Don't try to slice meat off, but scrape it off with blade and pulling.

Alternate methods

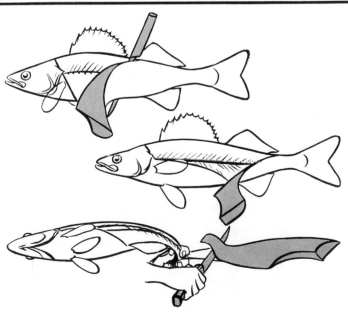

After removing entrails, make cut just behind head. Slice along backbone through rib cage and body cavity, but don't cut through skin at tail. Separate skin and meat as shown below. Rib bones can be sliced from fillet.

Start by slicing the fillet at back and dorsal. When knife strikes rib cage work to outside, slice off. There's more meat loss but it's quicker. Behind vent area continue cutting to tail at full depth. Don't cut skin at tail.

With the fillet still connected to body at tail, flip meat skin down on table and use tail as handle while skinning fillet (Step 4 above).

Fillets of fresh salmon broiling over an open fire on the beach top off this trip

Broiling—*On a plank*

One method for broiling a fish over an open fire utilizes a split log or wooden slab 2 or more inches thick. Split the fish down the back, leaving the belly intact. Cut off head, fins, and remove entrails. Spread the fish on the plank skin down and tack it with hardwood pegs or nails. Rub salt and butter into meat, or baste with bacon when hot.

Prop log up near flaming fire but not close enough to burn. Plank should be turned end for end occasionally to give an even broiling. Test with a fork; meat will flake when done.

Baking—*Use of foil*

An easy way of cooking fish is by using aluminum foil and hot coals of campfire. Lay fillet on a sheet of heavy foil making sure backbone does not poke a hole. On top the fillet place a layer of thin-sliced potatoes, a small bit of onion, if desired, (too much spoils fish flavor) and a generous slab of butter. Top with another fillet and wrap carefully into tight roll, folding ends and top securely.

Lay foil on coals, turning at least once to cook evenly. Cooking time runs about 30 minutes. Unfold foil and test for flaking.

Chapter 8

How to cook fish

Campfire cooking

Frying

A simple cooking method is to fry fish in a heavy cast iron skillet. Clean fish, wipe nearly dry, then flour with corn meal, pancake mix, or packaged biscuit mix. Flour fish by shaking in paper sack. If a batter of eggs and milk is used, dip fish in cracker or bread crumbs.

Use oil, shortening, or butter about ¼ inch deep in skillet, preheating until hot, but not smoking, or until a bit of bread browns quickly. As soon as fish browns on one side, turn over. When it flakes with fork remove from skillet, drain on absorbent paper.

Fish Chowder

In a deep pan, fry until crisp 3 or 4 slices of chopped-up bacon. Add 1 or 2 onions, 2 cups of sliced potatoes, 1 teaspoon salt, and 4 cups water. Bring to boil and simmer for 10 to 15 minutes. When potatoes are nearly soft put in about 2 pounds of cubed fillets with bones removed. Cook fish until tender, about 15 minutes; add 4 cups evaporated milk. (Or use powdered milk pre-mixed in water and reduce water used to boil potatoes.) Add a generous chunk of butter, bring just to boil and simmer until hot through. Salt and pepper to taste.

Smoking fish

Smoking is one of the oldest methods of preparing fish. Originally used as a means of preserving fish in the days before refrigeration, smoking is now popular because it produces excellent flavor and turns the meat of less desirable fish—such as carp and suckers—into enjoyable food.

The two basic methods of smoking fish are hot or cold smoking. In hot smoking, the fish is cooked and flavored at temperatures of 160 to 180 degrees Fahrenheit for 4 to 14 or more hours. In cold smoking, the fish is not cooked but dried at 90-degrees temperature for one to six days. The hot smoking method is most popular with fishermen because it requires less time.

Many types of smokers can be used; a wooden barrel, steel drum, even a discarded icebox will produce excellent results. The smoker must have vents to provide smoke and fresh air circulation and must have racks, trays, or hooks for holding the meat. Ventilation should be controlled so the fuel smolders but does not flame, and to hold an even temperature.

Clean fish thoroughly before smoking

Prior to smoking, clean fish as usual, but do not remove skin. If trays are used, the fish can be split and placed skin-down in smoker.

Before the fish can be smoked it should be cured. One method uses a salt brine containing 4 cups of salt, 2 cups brown sugar, 2 tablespoons black pepper, and 2 tablespoons crushed bay leaves. Or a brine can be made simply by adding salt to water. Usually, if the brine contains enough salt to float an egg it is strong enough.

The cleaned fish is placed in the brine and left anywhere from two hours to overnight depending upon the degree of curing desired. When fish are removed from the brine, they are rinsed in cold water, then dried on screens or by hanging in a cool shady spot for about three hours or until a shiny skin forms on meat. Be certain fish are dry before placing them in smoker.

Alternate method of curing fish

Another method of preparing cleaned fish for smoking is simply to rub them liberally with salt and pack them together in a box, scattering more salt over the fish as they are packed. After curing, remove the fish from the box and smoke in same manner as with brine-cured fish.

The length of time for the actual smoking process will vary depending upon the size of the fish, the amount of smoke flavor the angler prefers and the heat inside the smoker. The meat should be taste-tested occasionally and removed from the smoker when it reaches the desired flavor. Hot smoked fish need refrigeration.

Use non-resinous wood for fuel. Oak, hickory, maple, beech, alder, vine maple, and all dry fruit woods are good for fuel. Hardwood chips or sawdust are used by many people. Corncobs can be used, but they're inclined to flame if not watched carefully. Several charcoal briquets can be added to the fire to keep it smoking evenly. Some experts use an electric or gas plate for a heat source and place a pan of dampened sawdust over the heat to create smoke.

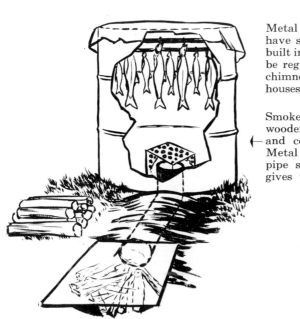

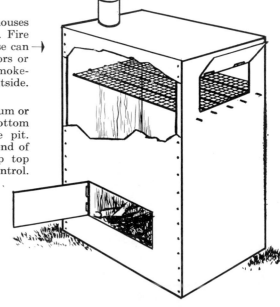

Metal or wooden smokehouses have screened trays for fish. Fire built inside metal smokehouse can → be regulated by opening doors or chimney damper. Wooden smokehouses should have fire pit outside.

Smokehouse can be an oil drum or wooden barrel. Cut hole in bottom ← and connect pipe from fire pit. Metal box with holes over end of pipe spreads smoke. Burlap top gives ventilation, smoke control.

Cooking at home

The basic rules for cooking fish are few and easy to follow, even though each type of fish has individual flavor, texture, and appearance.

If you make allowances for the fat content of fish, you can successfully use any of the cooking methods for almost all species. In other words, *lean* fish may be cooked by dry heat methods such as baking or broiling, if you baste frequently with melted butter or shortening to prevent drying. (Try combining lemon or garlic with the basting fat, or using a basting sauce.) Fish with high fat content don't have to be basted.

Avoid overcooking fish. It should be moist and tender with a delicate flavor. Overcooking causes the fish to become increasingly dry and chewy. Fish is done when the flesh is translucent and can be easily flaked with a fork.

Three basic cuts of fish

Dressed, or pan-dressed
Scaled, drawn with head, tail, and fins removed.

Steaked
Cross-sectional slices are cut from larger fish.

Filleted
Sides of fish are cut lengthwise along backbone.

Don't overhandle the fish during cooking and serving. Cooked fish is delicate and will flake apart easily. Turn only once during cooking and transfer carefully to a warm platter to serve. Never leave fresh fish soaking in water. This causes loss of flavor and makes the flesh flabby. Wash fish quickly, drain, and dry carefully on paper toweling.

Broiling

Sprinkle serving-sized portions of fish with salt and pepper. Place on preheated greased broiler pan, skin side up if skin has not been removed from fillets. Brush with melted butter. Broil about 2 inches from heat 5 to 8 minutes, or till fish flakes easily with a fork.

Baking

Rub cleaned fish inside and out with salt; place in a greased baking pan. Brush with melted fat (lay slices of bacon over top if desired). Bake in a moderate oven till fish flakes easily with a fork. If fish seems dry while baking, baste with drippings.

Steaming

Salt cleaned fish on both sides. Place fish in a well-greased steamer pan and cook over boiling water till fish flakes easily with a fork. Serve at once with lemon or a sauce.

Deep fat frying

Sprinkle serving-sized portions of fish with salt and pepper. Dip fish in mixture of 1 tablespoon milk to 1 egg. Roll in bread or cracker crumbs, cornmeal, or flour. Cook fish in deep fat (375°) till golden brown. Drain on absorbent paper. Serve with lemon or sauce.

Note: For frying, planking, or poaching fish, see recipes on the following pages.

Recipes

Trout Amandine

4 brook trout, cleaned (or crappies,
  bluegills, or yellow perch)
Seasoned flour
½ cup butter
2 tablespoons slivered almonds
¼ cup lemon juice
2 tablespoons snipped parsley

Remove heads from fish; wash; dry. Dip in seasoned flour. Melt ¼ cup of the butter; add fish and fry 12 to 15 minutes, till browned and fish flakes; turn once. Remove from pan and keep warm.

Melt remaining butter in skillet; mixing with crusty bits. Add almonds; brown, stirring occasionally. Stir in lemon juice and parsley; season. Pour over fish. Serves 4.

Broiled Lake Trout

6 1-inch-thick lake trout steaks (or
  use northern, muskie, or salmon)
⅓ cup butter, melted
Salt and pepper
Caper Sauce

Preheat broiler with broiler pan removed. Place fish steaks on greased broiler pan. Brush with melted butter and season. Broil about 2 inches from heat for 5 minutes. Turn; brush with melted butter, and broil 3 minutes longer or till fish flakes. Serve immediately with Caper Sauce, lemon wedges. If desired, trim with olive kabobs.

Caper Sauce

Dry ¼ cup drained chopped pickle and 2 tablespoons drained finely chopped capers on paper towels. Add to 1 cup mayonnaise. Stir in 1½ teaspoons each prepared mustard and snipped parsley.

Planked Stuffed Walleye

1 3-pound walleye or pike, cleaned
⅓ cup chopped celery
2 tablespoons chopped onion
1½ teaspoons minced parsley
2 cups dry bread cubes
½ teaspoon salt and dash pepper
½ teaspoon sage or marjoram
• • •
Melted butter
4 slices bacon
3 ripe tomatoes, cut in half
Duchess Potatoes
2 10-ounce packages frozen peas,
  cooked and drained

Wash fish; remove head, fins, and backbone, but leave tail on. Wipe dry. Rub inside and out with salt. Let stand 10 minutes.

Cook celery, onion, and parsley in 2 tablespoons hot fat till just tender. Combine with bread cubes and seasonings. Toss lightly. Stuff fish loosely. Skewer; lace.

Upper left: Trout Amandine *Lower left:* Broiled Lake Trout with Caper Sauce *Lower r*

Place fish on seasoned plank or well-greased bake-and-serve platter. Brush fish with melted butter. Bake uncovered at 375° for 25 minutes. Remove from oven.

Lay bacon strips over fish. Place tomato halves beside fish and brush cut surfaces with garlic salad dressing. Pipe Duchess Potatoes around edge of plank. Return to oven for 15 minutes or till fish flakes.

To serve, remove skewers; add peas to remaining space on plank. Makes 6 servings.

Duchess Potatoes

4 cups hot mashed potatoes
1 tablespoon butter
2 beaten egg yolks
2 tablespoons butter, melted

Combine first 3 ingredients; add salt and white pepper to taste; mix well. Using pastry bag with No. 7 or 9 star tip, pipe around edge of plank. Drizzle with melted butter. Bake at 375° for 15 minutes.

Poached Salmon

1 4- to 5-pound salmon, cleaned
Water to cover*
For each *quart* of water, add:
½ medium onion, sliced
1 tablespoon vinegar
1½ teaspoons pickling spice
1½ teaspoons salt
½ teaspoon whole black peppers
1 bay leaf

• • •

Cucumber Sauce

Remove head and tail from salmon. Wash. Wrap carefully in cheesecloth.

In oval roaster, fish cooker, or other pan large enough to accommodate salmon, combine warm water, onion, vinegar, and spices. Bring to boiling.

Place salmon in the boiling water. Cover and simmer 25 to 30 minutes or till salmon just flakes. Using cheesecloth as a sling, remove salmon to a baking sheet. Cool.

Carefully peel off top skin. Turn over onto serving platter, using cheesecloth as a guide. Discard cheesecloth. Remove remaining skin. Chill salmon thoroughly.

Serve on bed of water cress; tuck in halved cherry tomatoes if desired. Atop salmon, parade notched halved lemon slices and thin cucumber slices. Serve on buffet with Cucumber Sauce. Serves 16 to 20.

*To measure water, place salmon in pan and pour warm water over. Then remove fish while warm water comes to a boil.

Cucumber Sauce

After saving a few slices to trim fish, cut one medium unpared cucumber in half lengthwise; scoop out seeds. Grate cucumber (you'll need about 1 cup grated); drain. Combine ½ cup dairy sour cream, ¼ cup mayonnaise, 1 tablespoon grated onion and minced parsley, 2 teaspoons vinegar, and ¼ teaspoon salt *each*. Add cucumber. Chill. Makes about 1½ cups.

...ked Stuffed Walleye with Duchess Potatoes   *Upper right: Poached Salmon with Cucumber Sauce*

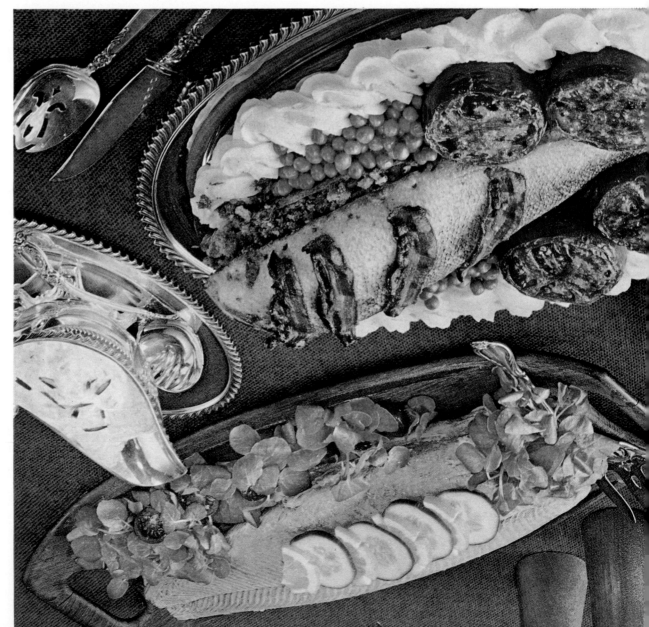

Picture credits

Photos by Maynard Reece unless otherwise indicated

8.....Jim Sherman
11.....Jim Sherman, Bill Browning,
        Jim Sherman
14.....Ira Spring
15.....Ries Tuttle
18.....Ver Keljik
19.....Ver Keljik, Clark Dean
21.....Don Wooldridge
22.....Bill Browning
23.....Don Wooldridge, Charles Schwartz,
        Bill Browning
36.....Henry Bradshaw
44.....Jim Sherman
45.....Hank Andrews
48.....George Sand
50.....Howard Gray, Don Wooldridge
51.....Erwin A. Bauer
54.....Erwin A. Bauer
72.....Don Wooldridge, Allen Snook,
        Bill Browning
73.....Howard Gray
78.....Johnnie M. Gray
81.....Henry Bradshaw
87.....George Sand
91.....Canadian Film Board
92.....Canadian Film Board
96.....Ross Hall
97.....Howard Gray
100.....Canadian Film Board
101.....Robert Elliot
102.....Henry Bradshaw
105.....Bill Browning
108.....Ross Hall
109.....Howard Gray
110.....Josef Muench

114.....Jim Simon
119.....New Hampshire Fish & Game Dept.
125.....Ries Tuttle
128.....Enos Bradner
131.....Bill Browning
132.....Jan Fardell
135.....Holden Hayden
139.....Canadian Film Board
141.....Leonard Lee Rue III
148.....Jim Sherman
153.....Jim Sherman
155.....Erwin A. Bauer
159.....Jim Sherman
163.....Erwin A. Bauer
165.....Henry Bradshaw
166.....Don Wooldridge
169.....Don Wooldridge
176.....Henry Bradshaw
177.....Henry Bradshaw
179.....Henry Bradshaw
181.....Vacationland Studio, Jim Sherman
182.....Jim Sherman
191.....Hank Andrews
192.....George Sand
193.....Erwin A. Bauer, Bill Browning
194.....Erwin A. Bauer
195.....Erwin A. Bauer
196.....Erwin A. Bauer, Henry Bradshaw
203.....Don Wooldridge
205.....Henry Bradshaw
206.....Don Wooldridge
209.....Ries Tuttle
214.....Erwin A. Bauer
218.....Allen Snook

Index

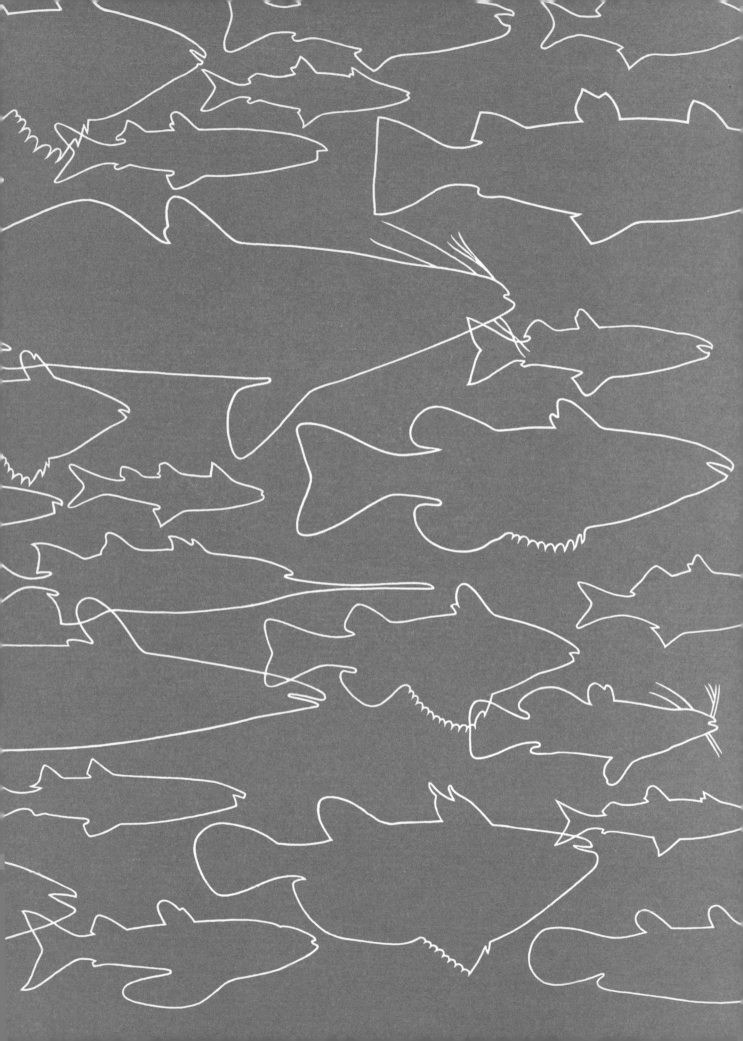